D0119726

STRICTLY CLASSIFIED

MARTEN JULIAN

STRICTLY CLASSIFIED

INSIGHTS INTO THE TRAINER'S MIND

RACING POST

Published in 2015
by Racing Post Books
27 Kingfisher Court, Hambridge Road, Newbury, Berkshire, RG14 5SJ

10 9 8 7 6 5 4 3 2 1

ISBN 978-1-909471-53-5

Cover designed by Jay Vincent

Typeset by J Schwartz & Co

Printed and bound in the UK by CPI Group (UK) Ltd, Croydon, CR0 4YY

www.racingpost.com/shop

To Declan Murphy

The inspiration for this book

Contents

Acknowledgements

Writing this book has been an interesting, illuminating, demanding and satisfying project. It brought new people into my life, and re-affirmed the value and importance of those already there.

Their brief mention here is regretfully inadequate in relation to the size of their contribution.

The inspiration for this book came from ex-jockey Declan Murphy, a man of great insight and perception, who ignited the flame with those few words many years ago at the Newmarket Sales – 'the spirit of this horse has been broken'. We must never forget our teachers, and nobody has taught me more about the mind of the racehorse than Declan.

The book would not have been possible without the support and encouragement of James de Wesselow, who believed in this project from my first pitch and duly commissioned it during his time as Managing Director of Racing Post Books and Raceform Ltd. Since his departure Julian Brown and James Norris have guided us all through to the production stage.

I am immensely grateful to the two 'Ians' – Preece and Greensill – who have painstakingly proofread my copy, spotting more than a few howlers along the way. Any errors that remain are of my own making.

Jodie Standing, my racing assistant, has driven me many miles to racecourses and proved an inspiration in her enthusiasm and extraordinary insights into this fascinating game of ours.

I must pass on a special debt of gratitude to Paul Day, who has been a constant source of encouragement and support to me ever since we first met, and Enn Reitel who, like the best of friends, has had the courage to tell me the things I sometimes didn't want to hear!

I probably would not be working in the racing industry had it not been for Brough Scott, who showed such kindness when finding the time to meet me as a student and then when inviting me to join him on *The Sunday Times*.

Racing can be hugely intrusive and over the years my wife Alex and our family have probably not seen enough of me. I thank them for keeping the home fires burning and for their individual contributions to the project along the way.

I would also like to thank the friends I made during my time at the Priory in Roehampton. Every day spent there was a struggle, but without that experience I would not have acquired the perspective on life which has guided me through this project.

This book would not exist without the contribution of the trainers, jockeys and horse people who have so kindly given their time to speaking with me and responding to my sometimes rather unconventional line of questioning.

Finally I am especially indebted to Rebecca, my eldest daughter. She has devoted all her working life to administering my business, protecting my interests and insulating me from so many of life's intrusions. She has loyally put in unsociable hours – alongside her role as a mother and wife. Without her I would not have been able to devote the time to this and other enterprises.

Thanks everybody, for everything.

Marten Julian

The odd couple

Introduction

It's not a lot of fun being 'stood up'. Mind you, back in the late 1950s, they didn't call it that.

But, as a nine-year-old waiting with my friend Raymond (see opposite) outside the Shaftesbury Cinema off the York Road in Leeds, the initial euphoria at the prospect of going to the matinee with Jess and her friend Sally steadily turned into a sense of quiet resignation that what we were about to save, in the price of two extra tickets, was never going to compensate for the loss of face.

As we trudged back up Osmondthorpe Lane to our homes – long after the movie had started – few words were said. We made excuses – perhaps they had forgotten us, or something had happened – but in our hearts we knew the truth.

I blame Raymond. As short as I was tall, he was a scrawny little brat – an urchin, straight out of central casting – and in truth neither of us were great catches. That experience, in the modern vernacular, would now be recognised as an early encounter with rejection. It was, of course, a very mild dose but I remember, even now, mulling it over for many days afterwards. Who knows how that affected my confidence, and for how long, but my perspective was all to change one sun-baked afternoon in 1969.

In stark contrast to the bleakness of Osmondthorpe, I was by then boarding at a school in the affluent south at Leatherhead in Surrey. One day a friend's father offered to take the two of us down

Derby Day – where it all began

the road to Epsom for an afternoon's racing. We found a spot on the inside of the track about a furlong from home, close up to the rails.

Those were the days when many thousands would gather on the Downs for the Derby, held then on the Wednesday. Although this was the Thursday of the meeting, there was still a buzz about the place. The fairgrounds were doing great business and my friend's father gave each of us five shillings (25p) for bets.

The highlight of the day was the Coronation Cup for which Lord Devonshire's five-year-old mare Park Top, ridden by Lester Piggott, was favourite. I did not know much about form at that time, but I was aware of Lester Piggott. Park Top paraded for a few moments in front of us before turning back to take the path across the Downs to the 1m 4f start.

I decided to place my entire bank on Park Top.

It was hard to see the early stages of the race from our pitch, but as the small field appeared in view descending Tattenham Corner it became apparent that I was about to double my betting funds. Piggott effortlessly moved the mare to the outside of the field, took a look over both shoulders, and eased to the front to win with any amount in hand. The confidence – indeed arrogance – which Piggott displayed as he looked back with disdain at his toiling rivals left me in a state of awe.

This was a man in charge, not just of himself but of the horse beneath him. Piggott encapsulated everything I lacked – confidence, assurance, style, class and masterful control.

From that moment I began to embrace racing as my special place. It was my haven. School life, just down the road, was pretty grim, yet a horse race allowed me the chance to do something with which I struggled in my day-to-day existence. It enabled me to express an opinion and, unlike so many other aspects of life, it very quickly elicited a consequence, with a tangible reward if I were right and a penalty if I were wrong.

There was a wholeness about it which I found comforting. It all made sense – risk and reward – and offered me far more control than had been the case all those years ago outside the Shaftesbury. It had integrity.

I witnessed the same thing with other people a few years later. I was working during school holidays at a factory outside Croydon and at lunch hour some of us used to wander over to the local betting shop for a change of scene. Here were men spending their days in

Park Top – the first love of my life

mostly dreary, mundane jobs who, in the placing of a bet, had a rare chance to exercise their judgement.

In those days there were no pictures in the shops so we had to rely on the Extel commentary, and if someone's horse was being called the winner the backer would shout it home, leaving us in no doubt he was 'on'. Racing gave that individual an opportunity to be lifted above the humdrum and monotonous tedium of factory life up to a place where, albeit fleetingly, he was king. That special moment gave him a feeling of self-worth. He was somebody, not just anybody. A winner.

During my time at university I stayed in touch with racing. Throughout those years I became increasingly intrigued by the racing mind and, more essentially, the mind of the horse itself.

Some years later, by then employed as a racing journalist with *The Sunday Times*, I attended Newmarket's July Sales in the hope of finding a lightly-raced horse with the potential to become a hurdler. I was not the best judge of a horse, but there was one which caught my eye so I had the lass pull him out of his box.

Just then, by chance, I spotted former jumps jockey Declan Murphy walking towards me. I knew Declan well, having worked as his agent in the early 1990s when he was stable jockey to Josh Gifford. From the many hours spent talking to Declan I knew he had a great insight into the racehorse, especially its mind. He wasn't interested in form or weights and measures. Driving back from the races he would talk to me about the character of a horse he had just ridden. About what made it tick. I asked if he would care to look at the horse for me.

He duly asked the lass to walk the horse up and down for a few strides before moving up close to his head, not saying a word. Thanking the lass for her time, the horse was returned to its box. We walked away and I waited for him to speak. 'This horse,' he told me, 'has had its spirit broken.'

I was entranced. What had he seen or sensed? Was it something physical, which anyone with a passing knowledge could have spotted, or was there a deeper insight at work? Some kind of alchemy, perhaps?

This book is not an academic study or a thesis. It is not specifically about the mind of the horse or its physiology. It is about the way those who work with horses try to understand them. Does it require a special kind of gift – something intuitive – or is it simply down to science and clinical analysis?

The gawky awkward nine-year-old in Leeds. The bewitched teenager on Epsom Downs. The winning punter in the betting shop. And Declan's insights into that horse at the sales. We are moulded by curiosity and first encounters which can affect every subsequent action. Those early experiences can shape the character of our lives.

Do these same experiences and emotions apply to the racehorse and, if so, how are they identified and resolved by those closest to them? I have spoken with trainers, jockeys, horse whisperers and stud owners for an insight into that special relationship in my search for answers.

Let the quest begin.

Marten Julian

1
The Broken Spirit

The spirit of a man can endure his sickness. But as for a broken spirit who can bear it? Proverbs 18:14

I am not sure how long I had been asleep. When I awoke the room was strange to me, the curtains had been drawn open and there sitting on a chair in the corner, legs stretched out before him, was a man ruddy of cheek with tousled white hair and hands steepled together in the posture of someone comfortable in the surroundings.

The Priory

'Hello Marten, my name is John Cobb. How are you feeling?'

'Where am I?' I asked, 'And how long have I been here?'

'You are in the Priory at Roehampton and you have been with us for three days, mostly sleeping. I am your consultant. You are worn out and need to rest.'

Gradually things came back to me. The visit to my doctor in Sunningdale had been followed a few hours later by the arrival at my home of a neatly-suited man with a briefcase. He had told me his name, but I was never to see him again. I do, though, remember his uncompromising and less than comforting bedside manner.

'Marten, you need to rest. You need to come to the Priory for a break.' His eyes stayed locked on mine. He never smiled.

'But it's the Cambridgeshire on Saturday! I have to preview the race for my clients. I would prefer to come in after the weekend. When would suit you?'

'Now', he replied. 'You have to come now. Is that your wife I met earlier at the door? I will ask her to pack some overnight things. We have a room ready for you.'

Now? Why the urgency? I felt well enough to work and hundreds of clients had subscribed to my services. What had my doctor told this man? The thought entered my head that, to quote the vernacular of their trade, I was 'at risk' to myself, or worse, to others.

I agreed with great reluctance to his request believing, naively, that I would be back to work within a couple of days. My wife Alex drove me the few miles from Sunningdale to Roehampton, where we were shown to my room. She helped me unpack, we said our goodbyes and I lay on the bed wondering what would happen next.

Within half an hour a ward orderly visited, pulled up a chair and asked me a load of questions, including why I thought I was there. That was a tough one to answer. By then it was getting quite late, and shortly afterwards a man in a white coat turned up with a small plastic tub containing a few pills. I dutifully took them, lay down, closed my eyes and was gone.

I must have woken at some point over the next couple of days but I do not remember doing so. My next conscious recollection was the sight of Mr Cobb, three days later. That must have been a Friday.

Cobb, for all his benign disposition, delivered his words with an authority that allowed no room for compromise. I asked how long I would be here.

'As long as it takes. Perhaps a few weeks, perhaps a couple of months. You are very ill.'

Over the next few weeks I learnt that I had been suffering from what is now called 'burnout' and depression. I would receive medication to help the synapses recover and a course of counselling to try and change what was deemed to be my maladjusted perspective on life.

Looking back, now 20 years later, that was probably the first time that there had been time in my life to reflect. I had been spending hours travelling to racetracks – there were no dedicated satellite racing channels in those days – regularly clocking over 50,000 road miles a year. I had thousands of clients, my *Sunday Times* column was widely read and my business had an annual turnover, on a good year, of almost £1 million.

The word which most aptly describes my feeling during my stay in the Priory is 'empty'. Something in me had been broken, but I felt nothing. I played mind games, imagining the most unspeakable horrors to those closest to me in the hope that it would stimulate an emotional response, but it never worked. I toyed with joining the Red Cross, confident that I no longer felt capable of experiencing fear, but Cobb would respond with what became a stock phrase of his: 'That's the depression talking'.

During my time in the Priory there were some truly enlightening moments. Most of the people I met in my section were high

Declan Murphy – the inspiration for this book

achievers or, if you prefer, perfectionists. One of the more common reasons for their being there was that they felt they had fallen short of their aspirations, in some area of their life.

Yet only negative terminology can accurately describe the dark times – there was an absence of being, a void. Whether that is what is meant by a 'broken spirit' I'm not sure, but my experience at Roehampton is one of the reasons why I could relate to what Declan Murphy had said that day at Newmarket Sales.

When, after looking at the horse for a few minutes, he said the spirit of the horse had 'been broken' I could understand. It is something that he could also understand from the times that followed his life-threatening accident in 1994.

When we think of the spirit of a person it conjures up something very positive – a kind of energy or life force. That is probably what Declan felt was missing from that particular horse. Declan would know more than most about a positive life force. In fact without it he would probably not be alive today. On 2 May 1994, the then 27-year-old was thrown to the ground at the last flight in the Swinton Hurdle at Haydock when his mount Arcot took a tumble. He was then kicked in the back of the head by another horse, breaking his skull cap, and it was clear from those in attendance as he lay on the ground unconscious that there was a serious problem. Swiftly transported to Warrington Hospital he was then transferred to the neurological unit of Liverpool's Walton Hospital where surgeons removed a blood clot from his brain.

Up to that point of his career Declan had ridden over 300 winners in England and Ireland and was heading for one of his best seasons. Four days after the fall he regained consciousness and on 11 May he was allowed home. To this day he still struggles to remember parts of his past – there are years missing – but his willpower and determination have served him well and he is now leading a full and flourishing family life.

Asking those who work or have worked with horses what the 'spirit of the horse' represents to them, I met with a wide range of opinions. There are those, like nine-time champion jumps trainer

Michael Dickinson – with 'The Famous Five'

Paul Nicholls, who simply say they don't really know what Declan means. Even Michael Dickinson, who among his other great achievements trained the first five home in the 1983 Cheltenham Gold Cup, suggests that if someone could perceive such a thing they would 'make a fortune at the yearling sales'.

There is, though, something almost ethereal about the way Declan talks about horses. His vernacular would not appeal to the pragmatist – the person more tutored in the language of science than spirituality – but there are many who can relate to his way of thinking.

'Looking at a horse is all about feel and instinct,' he says. 'Just look at a person's disposition when you meet them. If they have something on their mind then most people will either see or sense it. If a horse has something on its mind then very few people will realise it. All I do is look in the eye of the animal. Of course you can see things in the way they walk or project themselves, but you can tell so much purely from the horse's eye. You can see it in the eyes of a child. If a person is in pain it's all in the eye.

'For example when I was recovering from my accident I pretended to be fine but I knew that I could never disguise it in my eyes. Even now, when I get pressure on the brain, I pretend to be OK but my eyes show that I'm not. It's the same with a horse. The eyes can't lie. If a horse is a little bit precocious and above himself then you will see his eyes dancing in his head. That is a horse who doesn't know where to put himself. By contrast if you look at a good horse that is in form then you can tell from their eyes a certain calmness about them. If you break a horse's spirit then it is irretrievable.'

*A horse walks with its legs, gallops with its lungs and persists
with its heart, but it wins only with its spirit, character and
sheer determination.* Charlie Whittingham

Peter Makin, who started training in 1967, announced his retirement in 2015. He believes in the gift of insight, but says there may be a practical reason for a horse's apparent lack of spirit. He says: 'The Irish do have an insight into horses even though a lot of what they say may be fanciful. Declan was looking at an older horse and there may not be much juice left in the orange when one is sold from certain yards. He may, for example, have been used as a 'lead' horse – used to lead the younger horses in a gallop at home. Trainers would give their right arm for one of those lead horses but they do tend to be exploited to help the better ones along. That can break their spirit because they are always being beaten by another horse.'

Dermot Weld has scaled the heights on the world stage as a trainer. Since taking out his licence in 1972 he has trained the winners of 22 European Classics and almost 4,000 winners. His greatest achievement was to send Vintage Crop all the way from his base at the Curragh to Australia for the Melbourne Cup – a feat he repeated nine years later with Media Puzzle. In Ireland he has trained the winner of the Irish St Leger no fewer than seven times – on four consecutive occasions with Vinnie Roe – and has won the Irish 1,000 Guineas four times. He has also won the Irish Derby twice, the Irish Oaks twice and the Irish 2,000 Guineas once.

He prefers to start his assessment of a horse from his standpoint as a qualified veterinarian, trying to detect physical reasons for what Declan describes as a horse's apparent absence of spirit. 'I can't say what Declan saw on that particular occasion but I do know what he means. Very few people have that ability. Most people don't have the time to develop it. Others may have it but not be aware of it. Listlessness, rather than a lack of spirit, may be another way of describing what Declan saw. But then I would ask myself why the horse was like that and look 'mechanically' at what problems the horse might have. It could be a hairline fracture or arthritic problems that have not been picked up. The horse may have stomach ulcers in which case he is living in pain, so naturally he doesn't look so good. Ulcers are a consequence of stress and incorrect feeding. If he passes all these tests then perhaps it is a mental thing. He may have been bullied in the paddock by other horses – the weakest member of the herd – or been mistreated by humans.

'Having said that I can sense when a horse is not happy in himself. What do I see? Well, the horse's head may be down, even though we have done all the physical checks, but there is something else. The eyes and the head tell me a lot. Perhaps these days people look more at blood pictures but the eyes tell you plenty if you are very perceptive. A horse's eye reveals far more than people realise. They have more lateral vision than humans but I can see from its eye whether it is right or not. To sum up, I start with the physical side of the horse, then look at the angle of its head and then the eye.'

This all makes perfect sense to me. Usually there is a physical reason why we may look under the weather. The first step when trying to ascertain a problem with a person, or horse, is to eliminate the obvious. Only then should we look elsewhere.

I remember a wonderful scene in *The Osbournes* when Sharon Osbourne became concerned about their dog defecating in the house, so suggested to Ozzie that they acquire the services of a pet counsellor to try and address the issue. Ozzie's response was succinct. 'Take the dog out for a fucking walk!' He was proved right, and sometimes there is a very obvious reason for a problem. If so, that has to be addressed first.

John Francome, seven-time champion jumps jockey, author and former Channel Four pundit, is also inclined to attribute what may be perceived as a horse's lack of spirit to something more tangible.

'The horse Declan saw might not have been fed well, or travelled badly to the sales. He could have had any of a million things wrong with him. Normally you see it in the way their ears are set. The ears and eyes tell you a lot. Also the angle at which they hold their head, how their skin looks and the way they move. They are not all the same but you get to know a type. They will fall into one category or another.'

It is generally agreed in the racing fraternity that big ears are a sign of a genuine horse. An alert eye and big nostrils, to allow plenty of air through the lungs, are also looked upon favourably. That great racemare Zenyatta, winner of 19 of her 20 starts, tended to gallop with her ears pricked. I recall her ears flopping from side to side after she overcame all manner of trouble in running to become the first filly to win the Grade 1 Breeders' Cup Classic at Santa Anita. She was exceptional, and her demeanour on pulling up after a race was that of a horse that still had more to give.

Gary Witheford is viewed by many as a 'horse whisperer' but prefers to call himself simply 'a horseman'. He deals with the damaged goods of the equine world, notably assisting with the early days of a young horse. The term he uses for this stage is 'starting' rather than 'breaking in'.

He says: 'I worked recently on a horse that was a leading fancy for the Classics. When he walked into the yard all he did was stand in the back of the box, even though he was a very good horse. He had won a top race at two but had got worse and worse at the stalls. There were a couple of factors they didn't know about and he was fed up and sore, which is something I see a lot. Eventually they stop going on the gallops, up the yard or even on the walker.

'I had another – an unraced filly from France – that would not go on the gallops. She stood at the back of the box too and wouldn't

Gary Witheford – blessed with a tender touch

come to the front. She wouldn't even try and run away, just stood there with no character whatsoever. I did my work with her in the pen but as soon as I put the saddle on her she nodded, ever so slightly, which told me that she was sore. I rang the owner's manager to get her scanned and x-rayed and it was found that she had a hole in her tendon sheath.'

I have been present with trainers on many occasions as they conduct an evening tour of their horses. This well-established practice – generally known as 'evening stables' – varies from yard to yard, ranging from a casual look over the box to a lad or lass standing at the head of the horse presenting it to the trainer, who then stoops down to feel the horse's front legs.

One trainer told me that when he was serving his time he was told it should be possible to identify the individual horse simply by feeling its legs. That may have been the case when a trainer only had a few horses, but with much larger strings these days that seems less likely. Evening stables do, though, allow a trainer an opportunity to spend a few moments with every horse and have continuity on a day-to-day basis with the horse's wellbeing.

On the occasions that I've joined a trainer for evening stables I have sometimes been able to detect the character of the horse. I can specifically remember one trainer who was a bundle of nerves and almost every time he went into the box he raised his right arm causing the horse to cower away. It's not unlike people and their dogs.

Retired jockey Michael Hills, who rode over 1,700 winners in the UK alone, says: 'I reckon you can sense the spirit of the horse through its character and mannerisms. The way it canters or the way it goes around the yard. Sometimes a horse has nothing about him – almost like he's given up. It may not be obvious in his box but it can certainly appear when you race them.'

Dan Skelton, former assistant to champion trainer Paul Nicholls, is relatively new to the training ranks. He also links an apparent loss of spirit to something physical: 'It may mean that the horse has been raced in a specific manner, perhaps hard from the front and he's getting fed up with it, getting a hard race every day when he goes to the races. Full stretch the whole time. The horse needs to be freshened up. It should do less intense training, have a complete break and recharge and then enjoy a race and pass a few. It will probably look like a sick horse. It may look light and lean, wrong in its coat, head on the floor with a dull eye. It may come out of the box looking lethargic like it doesn't want to be there. He won't move when you run your hands down his legs. It has mentally given up because it has physically given up. You feel its withers and it may put its ears back as it doesn't want anyone on there again. There are 101 different ways of looking at them.'

Dan Skelton – one of the game's rising stars

'If a trainer says that a horse has "gone", then the trainer will be correct 90 per cent of the time. Most of the time they don't talk about a four-year-old being gone, it's a 10-year-old. He's had a hard life and been there a long time. It is very risky buying one like that.'

In my experience one of the most significant things that a person can say about anyone is that 'they have something about them'. That acknowledgement of something almost indefinable can be the precursor to a strong mutual attraction, but because something defies description it does not lessen in potency and this can apply as much to horses as to people.

The converse may also be the case. It was once said that 'the opposite of love isn't hate, it's indifference' and I have seen horses that leave you cold. If a horse appears to have fire in its character then that is something that can, with careful handling, be focused and controlled. If nothing is there, then there is nothing to work with. Some horses don't seem to respond to anything, almost as if they are devoid of character. Willie Carson told me that Troy, winner of the Derby, Irish Derby and King George VI and Queen Elizabeth Diamond Stakes, was 'a dull horse'.

The most successful horse I ever owned was Cloudwalker, who had spirit and character in equal measure. The best-looking horse I ever owned was Nisaal, bred in the purple by Hamdan Al Maktoum. He was gorgeous – almost too pretty – and although he did win a race he lacked the competitive spirit.

Roger Charlton, who trained Quest For Fame to win the 1990 Derby and has since sent out over 50 Group-class winners from his base at Beckhampton in Wiltshire, believes talk of the spirit of the horse is as much about character as anything.

'I suppose that Declan is really talking about a horse having a lack of character. Some horses have characteristics that need containing or channelling in the right direction, but in the end the horse is showing something rather than simply wandering about the place, never pricking its ears. You end up hoping that one day it will start to squeal and become a bit more feisty. There may be other things which have broken the horse's spirit.'

One of the best horses I managed was tricky at the start of a race. Mastership was a horse with a lot of class – he had what is now termed a 'high cruising speed', meaning he travelled well through a race – but he needed to be kidded along in the closing stages and delivered right on the line. We never really found out everything about him, but he definitely didn't like hanging around in the stalls for too long. On one occasion he was one of the market leaders for a valuable race at Ascot, but the occasion got too much for him. We had booked world-class jockey Johnny Murtagh to ride, but the horse virtually fell out of the stalls and came back tailed off.

John Gosden – one of racing's finest minds

I rushed up to Murtagh after the race as he returned to weigh in and he said, shaking his finger at me, that our horse had been 'very, very bad' at the start.

There had been another occasion at Newcastle when Mastership walked into the paddock as if he owned the place. Strutting round, taking it all in, everything about him was positive. In the words of my assistant, who was standing beside me, he was 'up for it' and he duly won.

John Oxx, like Dermot Weld, is a veterinarian and has trained many top-class performers including Derby winners Sinndar and Sea The Stars. He says that Declan would need to have been 'pretty psychic' to pick up on such detail, but adds he might have seen a combination of factors. Oxx would prefer to have the horse 'around the place for a while' to see how he behaved and reacted before reaching a verdict.

Trainer Ruth Carr, who enjoys a reputation for improving horses from other yards, also believes that more time would need to be spent with a horse before coming to a conclusion. She says: 'To be able to judge that from one encounter with a horse would be very difficult. I would possibly notice that it looks jaded or fed up, perhaps carrying its head low. Those are the ones that I personally like to try to help. Having said that, it's all about their individual personalities. I always think that if I can't see something that enables them to win a race then there is no point in me training them.'

I suspect that, like all of us, Oxx and Carr do form a fairly swift impression of a horse on seeing it for the first time. I can recall many occasions at the sales when I have asked a colleague 'Why do I like this horse?' Again, it is similar with people. We all form an impression following a first encounter with someone, and some of us will allow ourselves to be guided by it thereafter.

Newmarket trainer John Gosden has sent out winners at the highest level all over the world. One of racing's most eloquent spokesmen, he spent his early years with Vincent O'Brien and Noel Murless before setting up as a trainer in California. He is comfortable talking in more esoteric terms and recalls days when horse handlers regarded the spirit in a negative way, as something that needed to be removed from the horse before it underwent training.

'I do remember that in the old days they took the view that every horse had a sort of evil spirit which had to be exorcised in the breaking process. A lot of people used to think that the horse had a spirit and they would put a roller on as tight as they could and then the poor terrified horse would be sent off bucking, with the idea that you bucked it out of them. The problem was that it could do a lot of harm to the horse – it could hurt itself – and secondly many of them became petrified. The breaking process then became more complicated because the horse had absolutely no confidence in the people that were working with it.

'There is no doubt that we have found over the years that the more gently you break them the better. If a horse is frightened by what it is being asked to do then it may become cautious to the point of really wanting to withdraw itself. There have been horses whose self-confidence has been broken and destroyed just as with a human being. Some respond to affection, kindness and gentle handling. Others require a certain discipline and firmness – nothing aggressive, but just letting them know they can't walk all over the top of you whenever they feel like it.

'Vincent O'Brien was interesting at the sales. He didn't look at that many horses because he knew the pedigrees he was interested in, but he would spend a very long time looking at their faces, their heads and eyes. He was trying to discern their character, disposition and their honesty.'

O'Brien was meticulous in his attention to detail. For example, when his horses were travelling to the races he would always have a spare trailer ready in case the original one broke down. He would also have a reserve jockey for a big race in case anything happened to the first choice. When he thought The Minstrel, winner of the 1977 Derby, would be upset by the noise of the Epsom crowd he had cotton wool stuffed in the horse's ears – one of the first trainers to adopt what is now quite a common practice.

O'Brien was the greatest trainer of my lifetime. His record, under both codes of racing, is unlikely ever to be surpassed. He trained the winners of four Cheltenham Gold Cups, including three years in succession with Cottage Rake. He also won three consecutive Champion Hurdles with Hatton's Grace and three consecutive Grand Nationals with different horses. Then, aged 41, he turned his attention to the Flat and trained the winners of 27 Irish Classics, 16 English Classics (including the Derby six times) and three winners of the Prix de l'Arc de Triomphe. For him it was all in the eye.

Oliver Sherwood, who worked alongside John Francome with the late Fred Winter before becoming a successful trainer, thinks along the same lines. 'The first thing I look at in any horse is the eye. That can tell you a multitude of things. There is no right or wrong, and my kind of eye may be different to somebody else's. After the eye I look at the limbs and the backside. It's like looking at a girl!'

Some will argue that talk of something as intangible as the spirit of a horse, especially when it is standing before you at the sales, is more the stuff of blarney than sound scientific theory.

Dr Richard Newland, a qualified GP, trains just a dozen horses from his base near Worcester. His great day came when Pineau De Re won the 2014 Grand National, but he has enjoyed many other triumphs, each one of them with second-hand horses.

'Spirit doesn't mean much to be honest. I am being cynical but I am not convinced. Obviously I am used to seeing people dying in my role as a doctor, and being there when they die, but we are talking about horses here. A live horse, and we are saying that it has lost its

Dr Richard Newland – a master of two professions

spirit? If I can use the human analogy there is not a lot of 'evidence base' in racing. So when people say this is how you should train a horse, this is what you should do, that is the food you should feed it, that is the rug to use, this is the bridle – people are doing most of those things because that is what you were shown you should do. Peers and colleagues recommend this, and so on. It is not that it's wrong; it is built up from an experience base, but actually where is the evidence?

'If I asked your friend Declan Murphy to look at 10 horses, rate them all in the spirit from one to 10, my guess is that he would be right 50 per cent of the time and wrong 50 per cent of the time. I don't know how you do that. If Declan says it then we all believe him because it's Declan. But that is rather like the Professor of Psychology saying something and everyone listens.'

Luca Cumani – a non-believer

Luca Cumani has trained winners at the highest level all over the world from his base at Bedford House in Newmarket. I have known him since he took out a licence back in 1976, since then he has trained two Derby winners, a St Leger winner and enjoyed global success at the highest level in Hong Kong, France, USA, Canada and Japan.

One of the game's deepest thinkers, he has little time for metaphysical musing, preferring the pragmatic approach. 'I don't think using the word "spirit" is a very scientific way of looking at things. I am more inclined to believe science and facts than hearsay and black magic. For example I don't believe that humans have a soul and I don't believe there is a God. That is where I start from. I can't believe in superstition. I have, though, seen horses that were unhappy. We spend our lives as trainers trying to make horses happy – we change the rider or the amount of work they get. For example, this can be the case with horses that don't take their work too well and are much better following a simple routine. The bolder horse will adapt to a change of routine.'

One person who was converted, if that is not too strong a word, to the existence or passing of the spirit was Dr Sid Watkins, who did so much to improve safety in Formula One. During the closing scenes of the documentary on Ayrton Senna, the driver is lying down after his crash at Tamburello corner in the 1994 San Marino Grand Prix. Watkins says, in voiceover:

'I saw from his neurological signs that it was going to be a fatal head injury, and he sighed and his body relaxed, and that was the moment – and I'm not a religious man – that I thought the spirit had departed.'

'Disposition', 'demeanour', 'attitude' – perhaps this is simply a question of semantics, and we just have different ways of interpreting the word 'spirit'.

Or, as Dermot Weld and others say, the horse's disposition may be a reflection of physical discomfort or even pain. It may indicate something mental or emotional which traces back to its early years. The trick is to eliminate as many of the physical reasons that you can before moving on.

Yet I sense no magic or hocus-pocus in Declan's approach. By referring to the broken spirit he may, at a subliminal level, be detecting something missing from the horse's character. I have seen and recognised well-respected 'judges' at the sales in a trance-like state looking at a horse. I used to go up and ask them to tell me what they were looking for. They would say the usual things – a good walk, a big bold eye and a 'good pair of lugs' – but I often sensed that there was something else going on.

We are blessed with a wide-ranging lexicon, but sometimes the attraction a person has for a horse is nothing more than just a feeling. The spirit is intangible – that is something that we must all accept – but perhaps it is in its absence that it is most acutely recognised.

Ayrton Senna – a man of great spirit

2
Living in the Moment

If you want to conquer the anxiety of life, live in the moment,
live in the breath. Amit Ray

There are few things that brighten my morning more than the sight
of a newly-born foal scampering around its mother in a field.

Here is a display of pure joy, as the foal's delicate matchstick-thin
legs flick across each other, occasionally tumbling to the ground, only
to shake itself off and start all over again as if nothing had happened.

I once owned a mare named Rekindle. She was a half-sister to a
horse called No Bombs who was a useful dual-purpose performer
trained at Malton in North Yorkshire by Peter Easterby. She produced
more fillies than colts and most were born with crooked legs, the
dread of any breeder. But then, operating at the basement level, I was
never going to be able to afford to match 'the best with the best'.

No Bombs had an interesting background. He became known by
many in the racing fraternity as the 'Mars Bar' horse – a nickname
he earned following his disqualification from a race at Ascot after a
drug test revealed traces of caffeine and theobromine in his system.
It was later established that the source of the stimulants was traced
to a Mars bar that the horse had snatched from a stable lad on the
way to the races.

No Bombs was out of a mare named Land Of Fire, hence the
name Rekindle. Unfortunately Rekindle did not achieve a great deal

on the track – she did win a modest event over hurdles at Perth – and she was not blessed with the best of conformations, a fault that was probably passed on to her progeny. She did, though, produce one useful performer, a horse named Bee Health Boy who won seven races, accruing the best part of £50,000 in win and place money.

He was one of the horses that I saw as a foal one morning back in 1993.

My personal involvement with the rearing of the foal proved very limited. I occasionally drove across the Pennines when circumstances allowed to watch my mare and foal enjoy a pick of the lush late-spring grass in the paddocks. Polly, who ran the stud, did all the hard work. She was the person who stayed up night after night, fighting sleep to watch the CCTV anticipating the moment the mare was about to give birth.

Many times, now over 20 years later, I recall those scenes and still wonder why they felt so special. Apart from the obvious beauty of the occasion and the welcome of new life, I believe the reason it resonated was that it encapsulated the essence of 'being'. As humans we seem to spend the early part of our lives acquiring stuff, cluttering our minds with concerns and our environment with possessions and then, by contrast, we devote our later years to letting things go. So much 'doing' and no time for 'being'.

Yet here in the image of the mare and her foal is a young life, unfettered by responsibilities, constraints and possessions, simply living in the moment – not the past, not the future, but the here and now.

A Buddhist monk once told me that although most of us perceive time as linear – in a straight line – if you were to look closely the line is made up of a series of dots, each of them a single moment. The Buddhist term for the state of mindfulness is *anapanasati* – the discipline of focusing one's attention on the emotions, thoughts and sensations occurring in the present moment.

At stud – a touching scene

There is a wonderful scene in the film *The Good, The Bad and The Ugly* where the character played by Eli Wallach is taking a bath and an old adversary charges in, points a gun at him and begins what threatens to become a long diatribe about his grievance. In mid-sentence Wallach fires his gun, concealed under the bath suds, and shoots the man dead. Standing up to pump a couple more bullets into his victim, he says 'If you're going to shoot, shoot. Don't talk.'

In the case of the human being mindfulness – the ability to live in the moment – can happen in three ways. It can be a trait of the personality, for example in someone with a natural propensity or gift for it. It can be a consequence of something that has happened or, most commonly, it can be the result of practice and training.

The behaviour of the newly-born foal could be said to fall into the first-named category – some would say it's a gift.

Lesley Middlebrook, who with her husband Gary runs a private stud overlooking Windermere in the Lake District, told me about the early days of a foal. The best horse they bred was Reverence, who won 10 races including the Group 1 Nunthorpe Stakes and the Betfred Sprint Cup, but there have been plenty of other good winners along the way.

'It can take anything from 15 minutes to over three hours before a foal will be standing and able to suckle,' she says. 'It is critical that the baby receives some colostrum in this period to ensure they have a good immune system, so sometimes if the foal is slow to stand we will take the milky colostrum from the mare and give it to them by bottle.'

The moments immediately after the foal's birth are when the bond develops through a process called imprinting. The foal starts to recognise its mother mainly through her odour and her voice. The foal may be standing within half-an-hour and start to suckle, something that is instinctive in mammals. It may be making a noise within the hour and walking or even running in 90 minutes.

There are occasions when the mare may reject her foal. There may be a physical reason for this – udder infection is not uncommon – but the danger for the foal is that it will not be getting the colostrum it requires to fight infection. The foal is born with an immune system but is not born with any antibodies to fight infection, which puts it at risk for that period of time. The mare produces colostrum only once during her pregnancy and it is the first milk she produces but it is only there for about 24 hours. The colostrum will help the foal fight off any bacterial infection for about eight to 10 weeks, by which time its own immune system should be working.

It is important that the foal drinks and absorbs the colostrum within the first 12 to 24 hours of life. There can, though, be problems at this critical stage. Apart from an infection to the udder, the mare may fail to produce colostrum or may drop her colostrum before the foal is born. Or the foal may be too weak to stand and nurse.

If all goes well within a month the foal will be mixing with the others and be consuming pasture. Within six or seven months 75 per cent of the nutrients will be coming from non-milk sources, and this is the time when the foal is usually weaned.

Foals, both in the wild and domestic settings, are precocious developers and, unlike young calves that will lie in the undergrowth, they will be galloping with their mothers within an hour or two of birth. Initially they prefer to stay fairly close to their dam in the early weeks but by six to eight weeks they may be making trips further afield with other foals.

How soon is it before the character of a foal can be identified? Lesley Middlebrook says: 'Most healthy foals are inquisitive. In the early days their natural instinct is to stay close to Mum and be safe. Within two to three days they start to venture away a bit more and learn how to use their long legs, some even giving Mum a good kick. They vary from bouncing on the spot close to Mum – cantering around her in circles – to running all around the nursery paddock. Some can be quite cheeky standing on their hind legs boxing the air and are fun to watch. We had one foal born recently, by Rip Van Winkle, who is a little cracker. She liked to go out and bounce on the spot, whereas previously we had a foal that was very laid back and happy to follow mother around.

'We like to see character in a foal. Like the Rip Van Winkle – she has an attitude and is a bit of a monkey.'

Give me a child to the age of seven and I will show you the man.
St Ignatius of Loyola

As human beings we have the facility in varying degrees through the power of reason to address and sometimes resolve the unsettling and unpleasant experiences of our early life. If a horse encounters a problem it experiments in real time to see what will make it go away.

It responds to the 'here and now' and does not, in our sense, have the capacity for rational thought.

Belinda Johnston, a veterinarian who has also trained as a counsellor, specialises in the human-companion animal relationship and provides emotional support for anyone who has lost a pet. Johnston runs a charitable organisation named Our Special Friends, through which she provides practical and emotional support of the human/animal bond, especially in the elderly, vulnerable and socially isolated. She believes that a horse lives in the here and now.

'I actually see horses on an autistic spectrum,' she says. 'They live in the moment and are quick to spot something that is different. They can be spooked by something that is relatively normal. I think that rational thought is very much a human cognitive ability. I don't think we can say that animals reason things out, because they live in the present. A horse may be looking out of a stable door and suddenly their ears prick up as they see something that is different on the horizon. And someone with autism may not walk down a crowded street a certain way if there is something different. It is that ability to pick up a subtle change.

'Dogs do it through their nose. They have thousands and thousands of sensory experiences through their nose and with horses it is via visual acuity. They are vigilant and if they see something that is slightly different it affects their sympathetic nervous system and triggers the fight or flight response.'

David Pipe, son of the record-breaking Martin Pipe and now a successful trainer in his own right, has an example of this. He says: 'The majority of horses love routine. For example we have a couple of horse-walkers in the yard and we leave the doors open in case a horse somehow gets out of its box at night. If that happens we know that we will find it in the horse-walker in the morning because that is the routine it is accustomed to.'

One of Pipe's best horses was Well Chief, who was one of the leading two-mile chasers of his generation. He won the 2004 Arkle Trophy at Cheltenham and competed against the best around, notably the great Moscow Flyer. 'Well Chief was a special horse but he was very spooky and was quick to spot anything different,' says Pipe. 'He had a little quirk about him that made him good.'

A racehorse lives by a routine, generally imposed upon it by a trainer or handler. Horses have good memories, but their behaviour is not premeditated. They do not bear grudges and do not try to 'get back at us'. They live in the moment, and respond to how they feel at that time, just as they do when encountering a problem. In the wild, if an attack comes at a certain place then the horse or herd will avoid that spot in the future, but they are probably not consciously thinking of a reason why they do it.

I remember a documentary by Martin Bashir about Michael Jackson, in which Jackson tried to help Bashir dance. 'Dance,' said Jackson, 'Don't think about it. Just dance.' To quote a modern sporting adage, a horse cannot afford to risk 'paralysis by analysis'. A horse may, at times of alarm or fear, act impulsively but it will be quick to return to a familiar structure or setting in order to protect itself.

The challenge for the trainer is to allow the horse the opportunity to act impulsively while, at the same time, recognise its need for being around the familiar. One of the great joys in life is to see someone start to fulfil their potential, but that cannot happen unless that person finds the right opportunity to express themselves. A strictly ordered routine in a stable yard does not allow a horse to exercise many personal choices and, let's face it, the consequence of letting that happen would not be appropriate in an industry where young bloodstock can be valued at millions of pounds. As one trainer told me, if you put a load of colts in a field together they could 'end up killing each other'.

I remember one time seeing a mother and a toddler walking along a path. The toddler decided to stray a little wide of the track, venturing further away from his mother than he had probably ever done before. His mother looked at him without calling him back before he turned his head, smiled and then returned. This was an example of a moment when a boundary was reached, but not surpassed.

The key for the handler is to recognise when the time is right to allow a horse to express its personality or individuality. In the competitive world of racing this would ideally be channelled on the track, and reflected in a high level of performance. In the stable it can be done in more subtle ways, allowing space and time for a horse to indulge in its own little traits of character.

The challenge for the handler is to recognise when that time has come, and where the line must be drawn.

3

The Challenge of the Job

*Happiness is not the absence of problems; it's the ability
to deal with them.* Steve Maraboli

The lot of a trainer is not just about getting a racehorse fit and ready
to win races.

These days the job requires a wide range of skills – diplomacy,
people management, business acumen, the ability to handle a team
and, of course, the attributes to train and care for a racehorse.

There have been plenty of examples of top-class jockeys that
have either failed or chosen not to make the transition to the training
ranks. As a rider they were obliged to communicate with the horse's
owner and the team for a few moments after the race. They could
then retire to the sanctuary of the weighing room to enjoy some
light-hearted banter with their colleagues. By contrast the trainer, if
in attendance at the meeting, has to entertain and more often than
not console the owner before making the journey home for evening
stables and an early rise the next day.

There was a time when most racehorse owners were from the
landed gentry or highly privileged backgrounds. It was accepted
that the family's racehorse would be sent to their 'retained' trainer
without even a consideration for anyone else.

There were private trainers, such as Herbert Blagrave, who ran a
stable at The Grange in Beckhampton and trained only for himself

and his wife Gwendolen. He sent out Couvert to win the 1938 Royal Hunt Cup and won the same race in successive years with Master Vote (1947 and 1948). Blagrave only had room for 25 horses but had representatives at a high level until his death in 1981.

Henry Candy, who took over from his father in 1973, used to train for established owner-breeders – that is people who bred horses from their mares and then retained the progeny when they went into training.

'The whole game has changed but years ago my owner-breeders would fill a few boxes in the yard, mostly with middle-distance horses,' he says. 'I was known in those days as a trainer of staying types, but now I am more closely linked to sprinters because I get fewer horses sent to me and have to go out and buy 95 per cent of my horses. I try and find horses which are going to produce quick returns. It costs a fortune a day to keep a horse in training and very few people are going to want to sit and look at a horse for two years before discovering if it's any good or not. People want quick results. The sales ring is now king, while when my father was training there were plenty of owner-breeders.'

These days owners are drawn from every walk of life. The growth in the number of partnerships, syndicates and clubs means that anyone can now afford an interest in 'a leg' of a racehorse. I founded one of the first racing clubs, back in the late 1980s, and witnessed the enjoyment of people who formerly would never have been able to get anywhere near the owners' enclosure. Mind you I had to fight hard to get things going. The Jockey Club, as it then was, treated less than favourably the prospect of dozens of working folk becoming involved in what was still considered the domain of the rich and privileged. I was summoned to London to sit before a committee, who made no effort to conceal their disapproval of my proposal, but, through persistence and the services of a good lawyer, I eventually won through and the PSB Turf Club was formed.

John Oxx is also mindful of the commercial demands of keeping the show on the road.

'The challenge for me as far as the business is concerned is hiring the staff and keeping on the right side of the bank. As a trainer it is about getting the balance right between having horses fit and happy and enjoying their work. That is the important thing. I want my horses to be the best they can be, and that means maintaining the balance between hard work and being content – enjoying their work and not being overly pushed.

'Training racehorses requires keeping a lot of balls in the air at the same time. If you drop one of the balls then things can take a dip. Keeping them healthy, for example, is 95 per cent of the job. That's the most important part. You can't do anything if they are not healthy.

'The pure business of training a racehorse is to try and get that balance between how hard you work them and how happy they can be. The racehorse is an animal with controlled aggression. In that final furlong they have to stick their neck out and pull out that bit more than the horses behind them. They have got to want to do it and that needs controlling so they don't boil over. That's what it is all about.'

Roger Charlton is also aware of the economic realities of the industry. 'How many people have to operate in an environment where the business is not successful? If your food in a restaurant is not good then you get fewer customers and go out of business. Well the majority of racehorses don't win but the prices are inflated by injections of money from abroad and it makes it more difficult to make the financial formula work. The cost of training rises and the cost of buying a horse rises but prize money stays the same so the chances of being successful decrease, not rise.'

Trainers these days are under far more scrutiny than ever before. The *Racing Post* devotes a page every day to trainers' latest statistics and returns, entitled Signposts, which lists the 'hot' trainers – those in form – and the 'cold' trainers – those struggling for winners. The latter highlights the trainers with runners on the day that are out of form, recording the number of days and their number of runners since they sent out a winner. The figure regularly clocks into the hundreds, and the pundits who work on the dedicated satellite channels are not shy to share the latest returns with the listeners. Put bluntly, the modern trainer has nowhere to hide.

Yet the owner's choice of a trainer may be dependent on a variety of less obvious factors than the trainer's ability or latest statistical returns. This is something I learnt during my days as a racing columnist with *The Sunday Times*, when I was occasionally asked by a prospective owner if I could recommend a trainer. I soon learnt that people become owners for a wide range of reasons – not, necessarily, simply to enable them to stand in the winner's enclosure. Sir Mark Prescott suggests that for many owners the horse is 'an extension of themselves', and when it runs badly it is a 'public humiliation'.

But that is not always the case, as I found when I was approached by a top sales executive who worked for Mars confectionery. He was a man of substance and had decided that the time had come to try his luck as an owner.

Having ascertained the type of horse he wanted we then had to find a suitable trainer. Intriguingly, for someone who worked at a very high level in commerce, he was not particularly concerned about the training fees or the probability that the returns from prize-money would be modest. What mattered to him was that I found a trainer who could produce a half-decent bottle of champagne, at a moment's notice, and had a suitable area to land his helicopter on a Sunday morning. I duly found someone, now retired, who was renowned as a fun-loving sort of guy with a pretty wife and, essentially, a handy little space for the helicopter.

The horse had its first race at Plumpton, a popular little track but by common consent not the *crème de la crème* of racing venues. Yet that didn't matter. Standing in the paddock in the pouring rain, clutching his owner's badge, he said: 'I have waited years to be here holding this badge. You have no idea how much this means to me.'

The brief for this trainer was very clear, and it had little to do with economic returns or even success. As things turned out the relationship flourished, lasting for many years, and the horse did well and won at a fairly high level.

Perversely success can in itself lead to problems. Roger Charlton says: 'In my experience the relationship with an owner is usually fine until the horse suddenly starts to become quite good, even though that is what we are ultimately trying to achieve in the first place. If the horse is not any good the owner will generally take it on the chin, but if the horse starts to do well and offers arrive then they can become difficult.'

I experienced something of that when Cloudwalker, a horse I managed, won on the old turf track at Wolverhampton. Virtually every member of Equity had a share in the horse at some stage – the late Mel Smith, rock star Steve Harley and actor Enn Reitel, to name but three. On this occasion Mel happened to be filming in Wolverhampton, so he was able to pop over to the track to see him run. Our jockey, Tony Clark, was advised that Cloudwalker was a tricky customer who needed to be held up for a late burst. Contrary to instructions, Clark sent the horse into the lead and, to our surprise, he made all to win comfortably.

I was elated, but standing beside me Mel looked rather subdued. It turned out that Cloudwalker had been backed from 14/1 to around 7/2 and Mel wasn't 'on' – at least not to the extent he would have liked. It was only years later that we discovered the late Clement Freud, passing through on the way to a Liberal Party convention, had gone to the track and helped himself to all the juicy prices having spoken earlier in the morning to the horse's trainer Toby Balding.

I then had to drive Mel back to London for a show. To the day he died he harboured a grudge about the affair, convinced that I had been party to the coup.

William Haggas, like Charlton, enjoyed great success early in his career when he trained Shaamit to win the Derby. He says: 'I am always wary of the owner's friend. I see him as the trainer's biggest enemy. After Shaamit won the Derby the owner Mr Dasmal, a truly charming man, suddenly got lots of people telling him that he should do this, do that and do the other, and it put extra strain on our relationship.

'Now that I have been at it a little longer I quote Bart Cummings, the great Australian trainer, who had a fellow come up to him and say that he had been watching him and thought he was a marvellous trainer so would like to send him a horse. He asked how much he charged. Cummings replied: "Young man, I charge $300 a week if I train it and $400 a week if you do." If you get a top-class horse it can take over your life and you become part of it, but the more successful you are the less that happens.'

One leading trainer, when asked his greatest fear, said, 'An owner with a programme book.' Everyone agrees that the owner pays the bills, but behind closed doors many will admit that they would prefer the meddling ones to keep away.

Peter Makin is one of the Turf's abiding gentlemen. Diplomatic and polite, even in adversity, he works hard to keep everyone's morale up if things go wrong. 'It was quite handy,' he adds, 'to have a runner at an evening meeting as there was little time afterwards for post mortems!'

One of the most challenging times for a trainer comes at the sales. Standing at the side of the ring, there may be no more than a few seconds to decide whether to nod for another bid or walk away.

Every trainer has a tale to tell about being underbidder for what turned out to be a top performer – the one that got away.

Trainers will sometimes attribute their success to having one good horse – at just the right time – but as Charlton points out it can still all end in tears. He says: 'The sales are draining but they can also be euphoric if you have an owner with some money and you end up with a really nice horse. In reality you are then in anticipation of the moment when you are going to have to let that owner down. At least with a homebred it is not my fault. It may have a crooked leg, in which case what will be will be, but if I convince a friend that they should part with money for a horse and then we find it's slow, or has a leg, or can't breathe I then wish I had never bought the thing in the first place. It's just letting people down.'

Charlton's good friend Luca Cumani is resigned to things not always working to plan. 'The pressure of the sales is only because it

Mel Smith – my co-owner in Cloudwalker

Enn Reitel – my co-owner in Cloudwalker

Steve Harley – my co-owner in Cloudwalker

is very demanding on your time – from five in the morning until 10 at night for so many weeks. Unfortunately in this day and age you never quite get the horses that you want. The ones you want are the most beautiful, most correct and the best bred. In the end you have to make your judgement on what you would accept if you can't get the ones you like. You have to revise down and start accepting lesser walkers, lesser bred horses to the level you have the budget for.'

Peter Makin has been at the job for almost 50 years. He says: 'You have to look at so many yearlings and you might have good taste but short pockets. I try not to think back. I was underbidder for some very good horses, most recently for Lucky Kristale, who won four races as a two-year-old including the Lowther Stakes. I trained a half-sister and George Margarson, who got her in the end, also trained a half-sister so we both knew something about the family.'

Sales time is no different for trainers of jumpers. Oliver Sherwood, trainer of 2015 Grand National winner Many Clouds, says: 'Jumping trainers tend to look at the individual first and then the pedigree. The Flat boys look at the pedigree first and then the individual. At the sales you have to make very quick decisions in a very short space of time. Sometimes when a horse comes into the yard that I bought in Ireland I will ask myself what on earth I was doing buying that, but then you get to know it and it can grow on you. To try and identify its character at the sales would be well near impossible but for me it's a gut feeling with a horse. It's the eye. That can tell you a multitude of things.'

I readily admit that I am not the best judge of a horse at the sales. I have been told many times what to look for – a big eye, loppy ears, a confident and correct walk – but conformation is not everything. It has often been said that you can find fault with plenty of horses as they stand in the winner's enclosure after a Group 1 race. It is very much a case of beauty being in the eye of the beholder.

I remember a trainer once asking me if I had bought a horse 'at night' as the poor creature clambered down the horsebox ramp, legs all over the place, on its arrival at his yard. It was a tall, narrow, plain-headed thing that was bred to be a sprinter. He did win, eventually. A three-mile chase on a muddy winter's day at Plumpton!

But in my defence I have had over 50 winners in my colours, or those of my partnerships, and that is with very little money to spend. Money cannot guarantee success, as illustrated by the case of Snaafi Dancer. Sent as a yearling to the 1983 Keeneland Select Sale, the son of Northern Dancer was bought by Sheikh Mohammed for a then staggering $10.2 million. When he went into training he proved so slow that it was thought best not to embarrass his owner by letting him race. Given his outstanding pedigree the hope was that he would prove a successful stallion at stud, but he was found to have fertility problems and sired just four foals, none of them managing to win. He ended his days on a farm in Florida.

Paul Nicholls prefers to avoid the sales if he can. He says, 'I find the sales the hardest thing of all, especially the ones after racing.

Snaafi Dancer – not one of Sheikh Mohammed's better buys

I have owners to look after and I prefer to buy privately. You need an agent that is a good pal really. In France we spend two or three days in September and look at 50/60 horses and pick out what we want. I have a queue of people who would buy a top horse but you can't find them. Horses like Kauto Star, Master Minded and Big Buck's don't come on the market now and if they do there will be six people wanting to buy them. The market is as strong as I have ever known and it is very hard to find those good horses.

'The consolation is that jump racing for most people is a hobby. Like owning a boat or shooting and they will spend what they can afford. It's a dream. You enjoy the journey. Andy Stewart, who owned Big Buck's, couldn't even tell you how much prize-money that horse won.'

Henrietta Knight, a former schoolteacher and trainer of over 700 winners including triple Cheltenham Gold Cup winner Best Mate, says: 'The biggest challenge I found was dealing with people. Having been a schoolteacher I always talked to everyone but the most difficult part was dealing with owners who didn't understand the game fully or understand horses, especially the ones that would talk through their pockets. If I'd had the money and won the lottery I would have owned them all myself. I would not have had a single owner!'

The majority of horses that Jim Bolger trains run in his wife's colours. He says: 'My biggest challenge is to get really good horses – whether you breed them or buy them. Then, having got them, my job is to keep them sound, both in their wellbeing and constitution. Healthy and sound at the same time. A horse can be healthy but not sound in limb. If you get those things together then you are in business.

'The other challenge is that things can happen very quickly with horses. I could tell an owner that their horse was fine at 3pm and that we were going racing on Sunday, then at 4pm somebody else would say there was a problem. Human life is far more certain than the equine life because of all the things that can happen with the horse. The equine body is far more susceptible to disease than the human body, possibly because the horse cannot tell you where it is aching or feeling the pain.'

Although Ruth Carr operates at a lower level of the game she has done exceptionally well with the horses she picks up from other yards. 'I would say the biggest challenge I face is not with the horses but all the other stuff. Low prize-money, ensuring I find good staff and sometimes the owners can be hard work. My grandad loved the challenge of the horse and that was the most enjoyable part of the job. It's now red tape – medical records, insurance etc – but obviously the toughest part is to ring an owner to say their horse has been injured or worse. We have horses that have been in the yard a long time and we get attached to them. I suppose we shouldn't because it's a business, but if we didn't we wouldn't be human.'

Change the way you look at things and the things
you look at change. Wayne W Dyer

Luca Cumani believes the challenge of a trainer can be overrated. 'You make your own frustrations. There is one out of your control, though, that needs addressing. Everybody works very hard at this job but the monetary rewards are paltry. We have the best racing in the world and the worst prize-money. It would be nice if the industry allowed those who work in it to enjoy a higher standard of living.

'It's not as if the job is that difficult. Don't tell me that it is more difficult than being a surgeon. Owners and staff are the biggest challenges. Trying to get staff to do things the way you would like it done. We are not doing the same things now that we did 30 years ago, so I am always looking for lads that can adapt, but many of them are set in their ways. McLaren are not building racing cars as they did many years ago. They innovate all the time. You need people that are willing to respond to the need for doing new things. Most people are comfortable with what they are used to.

'Jockeys can also sometimes be an issue. I prefer a jockey to approach a race with an open mind and be prepared to accept my guidance. A jockey should never have a preconceived idea of the horse going into the race. That is the worst possible thing. I tell them all to have a blank in their mind and just do what I suggest. For example I don't want them thinking that the horse needs to make the running or won't pass another horse. I tell them what the horse needs. Horses, by and large, win from behind if the pace has been too strong in front and they win from the front if the pace has been too slack.'

I would be surprised if many jockeys will agree with Luca on this point. Tony Clark certainly used his initiative when riding against our trainer's instructions to win on Cloudwalker for us at Wolverhampton. I have seen and heard of many occasions when a jockey has kicked for home off a slow pace, or decided to 'take a pull' in a fast-run race, changing the game plan to suit the altered circumstances.

A jockey is expected to have done a little homework before taking a mount. For example he may ask someone who has ridden the horse before about any traits or hints that could help or, at the very least, he will have read up the form.

John Gosden believes the biggest challenge is to get horses focused mentally to perform to their best.

'As a trainer all you can do is realise a horse's full potential, and if that is to win a seller on a wet afternoon then fine. If it is to win the Derby on an afternoon in June, then fine. You will attain that horse's full potential if things have gone right for you, but you will never do that unless you have assessed the horse's ability correctly and, more importantly, have that horse mentally and completely in tune with your training.

'I can give you a good analogy from when I used to train at Hollywood Park in the 1980s. I was next door to The Forum, where the Los Angeles Lakers were based. They had a phenomenal team at that time – Magic Johnson, Kareem Abdul-Jabbar and Byron Scott – comprised of amazing athletes, anything from 6ft 5ins to 7ft 2ins, but they were like ballet dancers. So fast and quick.

'Their coach was a smart man named Pat Riley and I used to have supper with him after a game. He would say that he knew each one of his players was a phenomenal athlete and a brilliant basketball player with height, agility and speed, but he said he had to get them to play as a team and his greatest problem was to get them mentally tuned first to what he wanted, second to play together and third to compete in a really competitive way when they were under pressure. He said he could deal with sore knees and ankles and even their home-life problems but his greatest problem was mentally tuning them.

'When you are training a horse if it stays sound, which is always an issue, it has a level of ability which can take it to a certain standard. Then you need to pick the right race, the right distance, the

LA Lakers – a great team

Henry Cecil – a great man

right ground and the right jockey. It's important to have the horse mentally exactly where you want it. So, going back to the LA Lakers, there is no point in having these wonderful athletes if they cannot compete as a team and, second, if they are not in a strong state of mind. It is something that is very hard to quantify. A lot of it is done by feel. An instinctive thing, and one of its great exponents was Sir Henry Cecil.'

Declan Murphy recalls an occasion when Cecil landed one of the season's top Flat races with a filly that a few days earlier was carrying an injury.

'One of the greatest training performances I ever observed was when Henry Cecil sent out Bosra Sham to win the 1996 Champion Stakes,' he says. 'I used to ride out at Henry's and I remember in the days leading up to the race she had a poultice on her foot. They could not put a shoe on her, so she couldn't gallop or anything. Now there was not a trainer around, in my view, with the balls to do what Henry did and not feel the need to gallop her that week. He sent her to the races on the Saturday and trusted that she would be in her comfort zone and that she would be good enough to win. Most trainers would have put a shoe on and galloped her. If Henry had done that she would not have run in the Champion Stakes, but he knew that if he didn't allow her to be aware of her discomfort he would get her there. This is an example of a horse that, despite having a problem, overcame her fear. He trusted in her.'

Trust is a key word for Declan, both in the relationship between a trainer and the horse and between the trainer and his staff and riders.

'I used to ride in the States for Charlie Whittingham and I rode a horse for him that had disappointed on the track. I asked Charlie what he had done to improve the horse and he said he had not improved him, just found a system that worked for him. The horse learnt to trust himself and he won some very good races.

'I rode another horse which had been placed at Group 1 level in the UK. I rode him one morning at Hollywood Park before a big race and we breezed in '56 and change' over five furlongs and when I was coming back the assistant trainer came in and told me I had gone too fast on him. I didn't know what he was talking about and nobody else said anything. I was sitting on the corn bin afterwards talking to Bill Shoemaker and I could see Charlie walking around with his hands behind his back. He waited until I was on my own and walked over and all he said to me was, "Was that as good as it looked?" Charlie knew the horse was still in its comfort zone even though the clock said I had gone too fast.

'The horse ran in the Hollywood Gold Cup that Sunday. Chris McCarron rode and he won. Chris came to the barn that week and gave me $500 – I had never met him before – because Charlie told him about that piece of work. That is an example of having trust in the person riding the horse every day. Trust in that horse and he will trust in you.'

Charlie Whittingham – one of America's best trainers

Yet not even trust works if the horse is not sound and healthy. Oliver Sherwood says: 'The challenge is in keeping horses sound. The worst thing is telling the owners that their horse has a tendon injury and is out for the season. I just hate it. It happens regardless of your facilities. When 50 or 60 horses come off the grass in July you know that three or four are going to ping when you start to work them. That little bit of heat – I hate it. You can cope with most injuries and, even if it breaks a leg, certain fractures heal quicker and stronger but a tendon is the worst part of our game. The breed is weaker now than it was 30 years ago.'

Dan Skelton says: 'Injuries keep me awake at night. My first job when I am sent a horse is to look after him and try to ensure he does not get hurt. But if one does get injured it needs time off and that interrupts my training schedule. You then have to go to the next level and replan and this is the difference between the good trainers and the bad ones. The good ones are able to pick up the pieces and get them back on track. If every horse that came back in on July 1 never had an injury life would be a lot easier because they would all be very fit and turn up for their first race. But a good trainer can diagnose those problems, get over them and get back on track.'

Dermot Weld agrees. 'The biggest challenge is keeping the horses healthy. It's all about success. If you have success you will get the owners, I assure you, but you need to keep delivering the goods; however, maintaining the health of the horses is the biggest problem.'

Dr Richard Newland accepts the challenge of the job but doesn't feel quite the same pressures because he restricts his string at any one time to just a dozen horses in training. He says: 'The biggest challenge is keeping horses sound. Giving them the work and not letting them break your heart when one gets a leg or something. It happens all the time. This is a tough sport for thoroughbreds. It is attritional. We are forever retiring horses, giving them away or trying to find them homes. It is usually because they have got injuries and we can't justify carrying on with them. But keeping them sound and obviously trying to find good horses is always difficult.

'The guys who still keep them boxed are simply doing things the way they were traditionally taught so why would they want to change it? I do have a slight advantage because I haven't gone into racing with baggage. I haven't got a father who said we trained for

30 years like this. Look at Martin Pipe. He was an entrepreneur, who chopped and changed things and made things happen and if it was good he carried on and if it wasn't he changed it. In some respects it's not always helpful having people tell you how to do it.

'People in our business make judgements. Why are you doing this? You shouldn't be doing that! The horse isn't fit! But now having trained a good number of winners it's much easier. I have two very good grooms who have been with me for a long time and three work riders and an assistant trainer who is my friend really.

'People always ask me if I'm going to get bigger and I say not if I can help it. We all want winners and want to compete but I bounce into racing with a smile on my face and I see a lot of hangdog looks – a lot of trainers drink far too much and look under pressure. It's odd, because I go to work in my day job as a chief executive and nobody really knows if I have had a good day or a bad day's work, but in racing every Tom, Dick or Harry knows whether we have had a winner, loser, or on the cold list, whatever, and it is so measurable with everyone having opinions – 'that's a rubbish trainer, that's a brilliant trainer' – and then you consider the pressure of having to keep the boxes full and paying the wages, if it's your business and a living, it's a high pressure exercise.

'So as a youngster I had this fantasy of how wonderful it would be to be a racehorse trainer, pontificating and running your horses at the races. It's brilliant when it's working, but I am aware that if I keep it on the smaller scale I am getting most of the fun without all the aggro. When we started off I was absolutely shocked at how well we did.'

Sometimes the challenge facing a trainer can go beyond the traditional job description guidelines. Paul Nicholls, who has charge of over 150 horses, faced the biggest challenge of his career in the run-up to the 2013 Cheltenham Festival – and it was nothing to do with racehorses.

On the evening of Thursday February 28, Dominic Baker, the 21-year-old son of Nicholls' head lad Clifford, was killed in a road accident when travelling back home from work. These were testing times for Nicholls and the team, with that personal tragedy casting a dark cloud over the yard and the most important week of the season just a few days away.

'It was dreadful,' says Nicholls. 'Actually it did have an effect on Cheltenham. Everyone was feeling down and we had a poor meeting, with everything going wrong for the first time apart from one horse winning. When everyone is on a high things go well and it all rubs off on the horses. The funeral should have been on the Monday of Cheltenham week but we couldn't have it then and so during the week we all knew that the following Monday we would all have to deal with Dominic's funeral. We just had to carry on as best we could.'

How did he address the issue with Clifford? 'I told Clifford he could have as much time off as he wanted but the day after his son died he came into work that morning, went off in the afternoon to see Dominic and then came back to feed the horses in the evening. That was his way of coping with it. He had something to focus on and we all tried to support Clifford as best we could. Not a day goes by when we don't think of him and poor Dominic. He is an amazing man to have dealt with it in the way he has.

'I made sure Clifford had a proper holiday and arranged for the horses to come back in at the end of July rather than the middle. As a consequence we started the 2013/14 season a fortnight behind.'

Nobody is immune from pain, of one sort or another, and one man who had to deal with enormous physical challenges as a young man was Sir Mark Prescott when, aged 17, he broke his back when a horse he was riding slipped up on the flat at the now defunct Wye racecourse. He was in hospital for 18 months, during which time he couldn't speak, couldn't swallow or blink for a period of nine weeks.

'When I was in hospital I used to lie there and think that I would give anything to have the worst day of my life again. So, when I got out, I realised how lucky I was and saw that it was very very important to do everything as well as I possibly could every day but, at the same time, to realise that it was actually unimportant. In comparison to lying there paralysed it was actually unimportant. A couple of beaten favourites at Hamilton is not the end of the world.

'Although at the start of their careers most trainers are unqualified for anything else, at the end they could run a hotel, or a home for distressed gentlefolk – that would be for the owners! You have to

Sir Mark Prescott – a perfectionist attending to his affairs

know how to run a hotel, a business, motivate your staff, understand a horse's mind and make it all pay so you can improve the infrastructure and keep up to date. You need a million talents but I dare say that applies to a lot more businesses than we think.'

Prescott is renowned for his strict timekeeping, with accounts of him throwing buckets of cold water over employees who arrived late for work.

'One of the most important things a trainer can do is to come out in the morning at the same time, looking sharp and immaculate,' he says. 'Every day at the same time. The staff must be able to rely on you to be the same. However browned off they are, or how awful things may be, they have got to be able to rely on you as the person holding the whole thing up. It's all on your shoulders. If your best horse has broken a leg the business has to go on. Everything in life is a test of character. The only bit of the Bible that I think is rubbish is that pride is a sin. I think that pride is a great factor in motivation. But you must believe that every little thing you do really matters and that you have done your very best.'

Given that the vast majority of horses lose, every day of the year, most days the trainer is required to be the bearer of bad news. Sir Mark says: 'Some trainers will say the biggest challenge is imparting bad news and 90 per cent of it is bad news. At most race meetings there may be 100 runners a day, with just six winners, so 94 people will be going home disappointed. Sometimes in a poor season you are continually giving bad news and everyone is collapsing all around you.'

Peter Scudamore, now the partner of trainer Lucinda Russell, says: 'We are very fortunate to do what we do. Of course we have our ups and downs but our business is no different from anybody else's. I do think that with humanity the easier you have it the more you moan. Julian Wilson once said to me that to be a trainer you had to be 17 different things.

'I can tell you that as a jockey it was harder not to ride winners than ride winners. Victory is easy, defeat is hard. I never liked it when people used to say it was easier being a jockey than a trainer. They weren't lining up in a 17-runner novices' chase at Leicester that afternoon! I know it's not like getting shot at during a war but it is a very dangerous job, and when you leave it you have different kinds of worry. You have to earn a different type of living.'

Michael Hills rode for hundreds of trainers in his time and believes one of the most important attributes of a trainer is to know when to ask a horse for that little bit more.

'I still watch trainers a lot and the good ones know when to push the button. I rode for plenty of people and some push the button too soon and some too late. For example the horse might have turned a bit sloppy like an adolescent kid but the good trainers know when the time is right to move forward. I promise you that is the key for me. That moment when it's right to pick them up and do something with them. It is a fine art. It's important to know when to back off as well. Steady up with that one and put the other one on the back burner.'

I recall Dudley Moffatt, assistant trainer to the late Roger Fisher, telling me about a very well-known hurdler in the early 1980s named Ekbalco. This was a horse that needed to go to the races a little 'undercooked', as they say. Dudley, who in effect did most of the training, was away the weekend before the start of the Cheltenham Festival and, in his absence, Fisher decided to give the horse one more gallop – one gallop too many, in Dudley's view, and a decision that cost the horse the following Tuesday's Champion Hurdle.

The racing game, like anything, has its share of worriers. Something I like to do at the races is look at trainers when one of their horses is running. Their body language or demeanour can reveal their level of expectation, especially in the case of trainers I know well.

Dudley Moffatt – Ekbalco's guiding hand

I worked with Mick Channon, formerly a world-class footballer and now a successful trainer, for three years as his private handi-capper. He has a habit of lurching forwards, lunging with a couple of steps, if one of his horses is figuring in a finish. Others can be the epitome of 'cool', none more so than Barney Curley. I was once holding a conversation with him at Ascot while his back was turned to the track just as a race in which he had a horse running was about to start. Despite giving him every opportunity to walk away he continued chatting without even bothering to turn his head, still talking to me as the horses pulled up after the post.

Most trainers leave the impression that they are fairly relaxed – the smokers invariably light up – but I have also witnessed displays of nervous energy. One day at Haydock I remember seeing a successful West Country trainer – probably not entirely unfamiliar with the bookmaking fraternity – walking round in increasingly short sharp circles as his horse was running in a handicap hurdle.

There are many more potential causes of worry back home.

Michael Dickinson handled many of the best horses of his generation, famously sending out Bregawn, Captain John, Wayward Lad, Silver Buck and Ashley House to fill the first five places home in the 1983 Cheltenham Gold Cup.

'I knew I had five Gold Cup horses but in January they all went wrong and we had only five weeks to get them back to their peak. I lost 14lb with worry. Most trainers worry a lot. If you don't worry you should not be in the game.'

William Haggas has a more phlegmatic approach. 'I have learnt to delegate a lot more. I have a sign in my office, sent to me by a friend a few years ago, and it reads as follows: "Worry is a futile emotion." And it is absolutely true. Worry gets you nowhere, keeping you up all night. After all the owner and trainer are after the same thing. We are all on the same side.'

One way of handling worry is to ascertain from the outset those things you can control from those things you cannot. In racing a great deal falls into the latter category.

Paul Nicholls believes that the game holds back much of its mystery. He says: 'It's the unpredictability of it all. You never know what's round the corner. That is what makes it so appealing for the owners, staff and the horses. A couple of seasons ago we had five winners one day and then a few days later found that Al Ferof and Big Buck's had leg injuries. It kicks you up the backside.'

'The fascination of the game is that it is complex,' says Sir Mark Prescott. 'The reason that training is so stressful is that at least 80 per cent of it is beyond the trainer's control, for example when you gallop your horse you can't do anything to prevent it breaking its leg. If your stable is plagued with a low-grade virus for half the season there is nothing you can do about it but give the horses time and wait. What you can do is get out of it as well as possible but you can't prevent it happening.'

Prescott returns to the importance of luck, illustrated with an account of an event that happened in the dead of night.

'When my former employer Mr Waugh was old and ill and dying,' he says, 'I was talking to him in Addenbrooke's hospital – he was never to come out – and I asked him why on earth he had given me the chance to train and get all the owners to buy the place for me on an interest-free loan? All the owners stayed except for one. I was just 21 and I was the youngest trainer in Newmarket – by 19 years.

'I lived in Exning in those days and on one occasion I was woken in the middle of the night by the strong wind and thought the rain would be blowing in on the fillies in the wooden boxes. I turned over and tried to get back to sleep but I couldn't, so I got dressed, put on all my waterproofs and drove back into Newmarket. I got the window pole and went round and shut all the windows down the back of the wooden boxes and then I met him and he was doing the same thing. It was about two o'clock in the morning.

'And he said "That's why. When I met you that day I thought you'll do." Now I could have stayed in bed and he wouldn't have seen me, or I could have got there and he wouldn't have known I had been, because he would have done them already. It needed luck, you see. Equally you have to be keen enough to get out of bed and go and do it to get lucky!

'So I always say to my assistants if you are good every day you stand a good chance of getting lucky. Every day is a bloody battle for a trainer – and then some of them have to go into the house and start round two! At least as a bachelor I was spared that.'

Luck can take a hand at the sales. Prescott remembers the part it played in his success story: 'You have to get lucky every now and again,' he says. 'I got lucky again when I was sent off to buy a horse for Prince Faisal and Paul Webber and I were given about £100,000 to spend. We settled for one but he said that Prince Faisal would not be prepared to go over that figure. He said that he would fly over but he was very late arriving and the horse was walking round in the ring and we got to his limit and literally at that moment he arrived. He had been held up by fog in London and appeared as the final bid was being made. He decided to go for one more and bought her. Because of the circumstances he called her Last Second. She just failed to win the Coronation Stakes but became the highest rated filly of her year.

'Anyway, because I did well with Last Second, Miss Kirsten Rausing sent me a filly which was closely related called Alborada, and because Alborada did well Mrs Rogers sent me one which was closely related called Alleluia, so all that family came, including three times Group 1 winner Albanova. None of that would have happened if Prince Faisal had arrived one-and-a-half minutes later.

'Luck plays a huge part in everybody's career. When you hear successful people interviewed and they say luck had nothing to do with it I think it's absolute bollocks. Everybody needs luck and everyone needs someone to help him. Someone who likes you and gives you a chance. Those people for me were Mr Waugh, Mr Kernick and Lady Macdonald-Buchanan, who left all her horses to me when Mr Waugh retired. I can never repay any of those people but I really did my best to. I really did my best when they got old and ill to let them know how much I owed them.'

Dermot Weld sums things up. 'My appetite is still strong and the hope is in finding an even better horse from the younger ones coming along. This is a very challenging and demanding profession but your health is the most important thing of all.'

Dermot Weld – one of the world's greatest trainers

Nothing really works if the people and horses are not healthy. The knack for the trainer is to ensure everything is done to bring about that state of wellbeing – both mentally and physically – and it is an art that requires a multitude and wide range of skills, sometimes extending way beyond the mere husbandry of horses.

4

The Courage to Be

The worst loneliness is not to be comfortable with yourself.
Mark Twain

In psychotherapy self-esteem reflects a person's overall evaluation of his or her own worth.

I suspect all of us have been through periods when we start to think poorly of ourselves. It can affect every aspect of our lives, sometimes leading to the irrational presumption that everything we do will go wrong.

There are various therapies and ways in which a person can try to change their thinking and attitude to engender a more positive view of themselves, but that option is not available to a racehorse because it does not have the ability to reason in the way that we do. A racehorse cannot make the logical projection from, say, a sense of failure to a feeling of low self-esteem. Low or high self-esteem is a judgemental response to something that has happened, and that conclusion is a consequence of a complex thread touching on many other influences – most of them entirely alien to a horse's world.

Self-esteem can also be a consequence of the views and respect of others – something that is nonsensical from an overtly rational perspective in the case of a racehorse. A horse may, though, be aware of its status in the herd environment. If it is weak then it will be pushed to the outside of the pack and become prey to predators. If it is strong then it will protect itself.

This book is about the mind of the horseman, not the psyche or emotional range of the horse, but what has become apparent when asking trainers and handlers if they have witnessed lack of self-esteem in a horse is that it is not something many of them have ever considered – at least not in that terminology.

Jim Bolger speaks for many when he says: 'I am not sure that self-esteem is the right description. I would say that it is more self-confidence. I would not think that a horse is capable of self-esteem. I would say that the only animal with self-esteem is the human, and many of them don't have it!'

Returning to a constant theme through this book, the question is whether it is valid to attribute a horse with a human emotion – to anthropomorphise the horse.

Luca Cumani plays down the degree to which a horse can rationalise its feelings. 'Self-esteem does not apply in the same way to a racehorse as it does to a human athlete, eg, a footballer or crick-eter. Self-belief is linked to ability and a horse doesn't know what his ability is because he cannot read his *Timeform* rating. I would call it more a lack of confidence or shyness. Certain horses are less bold than others, if you like.'

Dr Richard Newland knows more than most about human emotions from his training in the medical profession. 'One of the things I tell people is, "If in doubt treat a racehorse like a horse." Everyone's natural tendency is to try and humanise the horse and think, what would I want? It is not true. They are horses.'

Dan Skelton says: 'Any patterns of behaviour in the racehorse are based on the herd instinct, not emotion. It might be nice for the last one to think that he is not as slow, but that is 'thinking' and I don't believe a horse reasons things through like that. I don't believe that a horse has a wide emotional range. The overriding mindset of a horse is survival.

'A human will allow emotion to get in the way of decision. Horses will not let emotions get in the way of a decision. They don't have the power of reason and their main priority is survival. Their instinct is flight, not fright. If they are offered the choice of eating their food or getting a cuddle they will choose to eat their food. My instinct is that if a horse is taken away from another horse, the one that is left will ask where the other horse has gone because they are supposed to be together, not that "little Jimmy has gone and I will miss him".'

Dr Temple Grandin, in her work *Animals In Translation*, argues that horses are incapable of mixed emotions, such as a love/hate relationship. She believes that animals, in general, experience four primal emotions – rage, prey-chase, fear and curiosity – and four primary social emotions – sexual attraction, separation distress, attachment and playfulness. The number of human emotions, by contrast, has been estimated at over 400.

Dr Temple Grandin – an inspiration to so many

Dr Grandin is autistic – she was consulted by Dustin Hoffman when he was researching for his lead role in *Rain Man* – and she says that her brain receives information in the same way as other people but rather than convert the data into words it remains visual. In *Animals In Translation* she argues that the frontal lobes of someone with autism do not function in the same way as a typical person, falling somewhere between the human and the animal, with an autistic person having a more detailed perspective. So whereas a typical person can translate an experience into words and abstractions, animals and autistic people process the world in a more sensory fashion, with pictures, sights and sounds. Grandin believes that animals have a superior perception of detail, as do people with autism.

Henry Candy can relate to that but goes a little further, believing that a horse lacks the intelligence to make the connection between its physical state and a feeling of low self-esteem. 'It is a hard one to answer, but you sometimes see a horse at the sales which has been done badly, possibly consigned by people new to the game who don't quite understand what they are doing. That could be a problem if it came into the yard but it's possibly taking it too far to describe it as low self-esteem. I don't think there is a mental state there. More a physical state and a feeling of unhappiness compared to the others. Almost as if they have been backward and not given the chance early in life. It is a fine line, but I am not sure that horses are that intelligent.'

Roger Charlton also sees signs of insecurity in a young horse, although acknowledging things are far better these days than years ago. He says: 'I have seen yearlings that have come in from Ireland that have barely had a bit on or a head collar and they feel threatened by a change in their environment. One of the ways they overcome that threat is to be more aggressive. Others turn timid, finding the whole thing rather awe-inspiring.

Roger Charlton – an eloquent communicator

'We see it less now because most of them have been to the sales as foals and/or yearlings and been on horse-walkers. They have had a much better preparation than years ago and what you don't want – and this applies to children as well – is a quantum leap in their environment. A horse can be knocked off its stride by being closeted away and then introduced to a boarding school type of environment.

'They are all different, but some want to try and take the system on and fight and get rid of riders, others are more straightforward. The main thing is that they are reassured by humans and become willing participants when they walk from A to B.'

There have been many examples of difficult or rebellious horses. Red Rum was so named, one story has it, because it spells 'murder' backwards – a reflection on how difficult he was to break in as a young horse.

The talented Tiggy Wiggy is a recent example of a tricky customer. The filly requires the most tender handling in the preliminaries to a race, as her regular rider Richard Hughes has experienced on many occasions. I was standing beside the walkway as she exited the paddock for the track before the 2015 1,000 Guineas. She was like a coiled spring ready to eject her jockey towards the heavens. Hughes was seen at his best here, saying to her three handlers 'I've got her, let her go, let her go' as he let his long legs, feet out of their stirrups, hang down her flanks. This was a living demonstration of the delicate balance between sensitivity and assertiveness – displayed by a gifted and very courageous horseman – in dealing with a nervous racehorse.

Like Charlton and Candy, William Haggas sees thousands of young racehorses at the yearling sales. He is less sure that it's possible to pick up on a horse's character at that stage. 'I don't know if you can tell something like that. I really don't. We don't break horses any more here. They go off to a breaking yard and then they come in and four to 10 weeks later they know the ropes. And the breaker will tell you that some of them are easy.

'Most have been prepared for the sales, virtually ridden away, and some take to it like a duck to water while others, perhaps home-breds, have been nurtured at home and take a while to break. The homebred that has been brought up on his own can be rather like an only child and doesn't know how to cope with the real world when they get to it. Then they come to us and you spend the next two or three months trying to get them to adapt to the system.'

Paul Nicholls is also aware that the switch in circumstances for a horse can lead to what could be perceived as a feeling of insecurity. 'First and foremost they are individuals. It can take an enormous amount of time to get to know them, but you quickly identify if one is going to be a little bit nervous or if it is more relaxed. It doesn't take long to pick up those little things. It's like someone going to a new school. Imagine how young kids react to find themselves in a new environment. Some fret while others cope with it well. Some would not eat for days. We

Paul Nicholls – master of his craft

try and pick up all the signs. Some take it and others get very worried. I'm not sure they get depressed but they can definitely go quiet. You do things differently. They can't talk and tell you stuff.'

I can relate to being a worrier. I envy the person that can compartmentalise, quietly put a concern to one side and carry on apparently regardless. A horse is incapable of consciously making such a deft mental manoeuvre. A good handler may be able to help it become more accustomed to the source of its anxiety, but a horse's character profile appears to be determined from an early age. In the world of the equine, nurture may not always be able to overcome nature.

Dermot Weld, calling on his veterinary background, believes that there may be physical reasons for a horse's apparent poor demeanour: 'Having first checked for everything mechanically – ulcers, hairline fractures, worms – if the 'MOT' is reasonable then it may be a mental thing. Perhaps the horse has come from an environment that hasn't been favourable to his confidence. Perhaps he has been bullied out in the paddock by other horses. If he is a timid sort of horse and been out with a lot of other horses perhaps he was the weakest member of the herd. Perhaps he has been in an environment where he has been mistreated by humans, although that happens less these days.'

Gary Witheford says that a horse in the wild cannot allow itself to appear vulnerable for reasons of survival. In a racing scenario it is different.

'I have a theory which has served me well,' he says. 'When a horse shows any sign of lameness at all it is probably at least 25 per cent more lame than it appears. That is because in its natural state in the wild it cannot show lameness because if it does then it will be at risk from predators. I think that horses which break down on the track do so because it has not been spotted early enough. So, in my view, if a horse appears to show low self-esteem then it may be a reflection of a state of discomfort.'

A friend of mine who works on a farm says that a sheep will try to disguise that it is lame when it is in a pen, where it may get caught, but is less likely to try to conceal its condition when with the flock in the wild.

What needs to be acknowledged is that a horse, like every living being, is changing all the time. This applies in its most obvious form physically but, with the racehorse, in terms of its ability. Luca Cumani says: 'The picture you have of a horse is evolving all the time. If you ever watched the TV quiz show *A Question Of Sport* there was a blurred pixelated image of somebody which they gradually brought into focus. That is how the horse comes to you. They arrive like a blur and step by step the picture clears in your mind and you discover how best to train them.'

What about the riders? Do they sense a lack of self-esteem in the horse? 'Do horses know when they have won? I'm not so sure,' says former champion jockey Peter Scudamore. 'I believe that horses learn through repetition. So if it repeatedly enjoys itself on the gallops then its self-esteem improves. For example I have horses that will keep running away with you, but when I put a fence in front of them they settle. I think that is like a bully or a 15-year-old rugby player who runs through his age group, but when he gets to play against men has to use his brain to survive. Horses will kick hurdles out of the ground and then you put a fence in front of them and it gives them something to think about. They realise they have to adapt to survive.

'When you are riding in a race as a jockey you can instil self-belief into a horse by challenging at the right time, especially if the other horse is going through the pain barrier and doesn't want to take you on again. But if you challenge him when he's feeling great in himself he will respond differently.'

Former jockey Michael Hills also believes the trainer needs to handle sensitive horses with care. 'It's down to the trainer to spot that. He knows that he can't put a lot of work into the horse because of the lack of self-esteem. They are herd animals and don't all want to be leaders.'

Peter Scudamore and son – representatives of a great dynasty

Henrietta Knight is a great believer that a horse has to have confidence. 'Horses have got to have confidence, like people and jockeys,' she says. 'Unless they have confidence they won't run well. A lot of horses lack confidence and it is the human element or perhaps the bullying by another horse that has destroyed it. We used to turn out our chasers here and you could always tell the one which had been bullied. It wouldn't thrive so well and would walk about a lot. Horses are very sensitive. The confident ones graze well and boss all the others around.'

Knight would not go so far as to suggest that a horse gets depressed or lacks self-belief. She says: 'I am sure horses worry. Depressed may be too strong a word. They appear to eat and look all right but sometimes they have to stay 22 or 23 hours a day in a stable. We never liked that which is why we used to turn our horses out in a field or put them on the horse-walker. None of our best horses would have stayed in. They would do something twice a day or go out in a field. But a lot of time now they just stand in their stables and nibble at hay and eat their food, and that is not natural. Stress is common in racehorses and many develop ulcers as a result.'

She adds: 'I don't think horses are as moody as humans. They are more predictable. You don't have quite as many surprises with their temperaments. We have had horses that don't want to go through certain stable doors because they are too narrow. There are box walkers which are anxious. Our stables are on a farm so we put the horses next to ones that don't box walk and the box walkers soon get bored going round in circles.'

Ruth Carr also turns her horses out in the paddock for most hours of the day and can watch them from her kitchen window. She believes that she can identify each horse's character from how they behave in the pack outside and can fully relate to the theory of a horse lacking self-esteem. She says: 'Yes, I firmly believe that.

Ruth Carr – always close to her horses

Some don't have any confidence. I try to restore their confidence by turning them out in the field because they are reverting to how they were. A lot of the ones I buy have not been in a gang together since they were foals and you can give a horse confidence not just by the way you ride it but by letting it find its feet and by giving it chance to enjoy itself. I have a gang of 24 geldings out at the moment, and that includes the better ones. There are one or two that don't fit in – perhaps one of them is a bit of a bully, for example.'

I am sure most trainers would like to turn out their horses every day but, as Luca Cumani points out, that is not always possible with colts and fillies. He says: 'Let's not forget that the majority of Ruth's horses are geldings. If I turn my colts out together they would fight between themselves to establish their level of supremacy. The same story applies to fillies; they soon establish a pecking order and may kick out, so that is why we leave them without shoes – to limit the damage. Also the weather in England is not always conducive. Grass grows in warm weather not cold and that's why if man didn't exist a horse would migrate towards grass. Warmth is what they treasure most.'

Paul Nicholls believes that Tidal Bay lacked self-confidence when he came into the yard.

I saw Tidal Bay winning a novices' hurdle at Carlisle as a five-year-old in November, 2006. He had been bought by owners Andrea and Graham Wylie for 300,000gns the previous May from former trainer George Charlton – a very underrated handler based in the north-east with a well-founded reputation for bringing along young stock. I thought the money they paid was ridiculous for a horse that at the time had run second, albeit with promise, in two NH bumpers but by the time he retired, eight years later, Tidal Bay had amassed over £800,000 in win and place money and won 15 of his 44 lifetime starts.

Tidal Bay was not straightforward, having a tendency to gallop with his head high. He often needed to be 'kidded along' in his races but, as with so many other horses, it turned out that there was a physical problem that needed to be addressed. He was moved from Howard Johnson to Paul Nicholls as a 10-year-old and had his first run for Nicholls in January, 2012.

Tidal Bay – enigmatic but hugely talented

'You could say that Tidal Bay lacked self-esteem when he first joined us,' says Nicholls. 'That would fairly sum him up even though he was an older horse. We had to turn him round but he was definitely like that. I don't really know why – he just was. His high head carriage was probably because he struggled with his breathing. He was quite insecure though. He would bite you in the stable and had a right old streak about him. He could kill you, but he's actually quite a nice horse once you get to know him. But he was very stressed when he first came in.

'We tried to do everything we could to get him to relax. The same girl Michelle looked after him and they trusted each other, but she is the only person who could catch him in the stable. He trusts her.'

One of the best chasers Henrietta Knight ever trained was Edredon Bleu. By the end of his career he had won 25 races, most notably the 2000 running of the Queen Mother Champion Chase, and over £700,000 in prize money. Life was not straightforward with him and when he arrived in the yard he was physically and mentally weak.

Knight says: 'He was weak physically when he came to us – like two planks of wood. He was nervous and very highly strung and didn't eat well. He had won races as a four-year-old chaser in France and been pushed a lot as a youngster. We had expected a lovely big robust horse when he came from France but he was narrow and insignificant.

'It took a while to get his confidence and he lived in a field with Best Mate, who was the boss, but they adored each other and became great pals. He was quite a nervous little horse. Very sensitive but he became more and more confident as his life progressed. In a bigger yard with loads of horses he would have been nothing. He loved to think that he was in charge. If we worked him with very good horses they would go past him as he was a slow horse at home. This would dent his confidence so he went out on his own and strutted about enjoying himself. He was as happy as could be. He was actually quite naughty to catch in the field. He would play around and not want to come in again.'

What does seem clear is that some horses are less self-assured than others, so how do the handlers address these issues?

Sir Mark Prescott says: 'If they are nervous with other horses you try and teach them to walk upsides with a nice quiet one to get his confidence. It may be accustomed to being kicked and bullied, so you keep changing things around to give it more confidence. A trainer is only a schoolmaster so when we observe these things we try and counteract it. When you have broken in your yearlings and April comes around you hope they are all good rides and will lead or go last and not be afraid. The winter is a very important time to teach a horse to become keen to please and content in its work. That is what the winter is all about.'

Prescott has a little trick he uses to boost a young horse's confidence.

'We don't pick grass in the paddock at home,' he says. 'We pick grass on the Heath. So that after they have cantered or worked they pick grass away from home so at the end of their work there is something pleasant and palatable rather than rush home in a hurry thinking they are going to work again. After they have worked the riders let their leathers down and like Pavlov's dog the horse immediately associates that with his work being finished and then we have a pick of grass and walk some. A simple reward at the end of their task for the day.'

'All trainers are trying to do is get their horses as fit as they can without driving them mad. There are a million different ways of doing it, but the common denominator with the most successful trainers is that their formula gets them very fit without unsettling them mentally.'

Roger Charlton also has a system he uses to help a submissive horse build up confidence. 'When they walk home from work I make them walk as slowly as the slowest horse. Walking along, chatting, chatting, chatting with the fillies at the back. If they jog all the time they don't relax and I constantly tell them to go slower because I want them to be relaxed. This environment at Beckhampton is relaxed so we can build a future for every horse.'

Henrietta Knight also believes that a lot can be done through the daily work routine. She says: 'There was a wonderful trainer called Ginger Dennistoun, who was John Oaksey's father-in-law, and lived nearby. I used to ride out for him when I was in my teens. He only had a few horses and he would ride out smoking his pipe leading his springer spaniel on a piece of string beside his horse. He was some character but he used to get furious if you let a horse walk too fast and leave the others behind. He said you had to keep them all together and never let one outdo the other one.

'If people are relaxed and there are things going on they will relax. It is extremely important. If it's absolute mayhem and chaos with people shouting that affects them. Their hearing is four times stronger than a human's. Horses are terribly sensitive to people raising their voices. They are herd animals and prefer not to be shouted at.'

Jim Bolger believes that the riders – those who work closest to the horse – are key. He says: 'The most important part of the operation here is the riders. You are better off having ordinary horses with really good riders than really good horses with ordinary riders. Riders that know their stuff can identify that a horse has a problem before it becomes insurmountable. If you are alerted to that problem you can change things and that is what we have been doing here for over 30 years. Of my 100 horses we would have a dozen that need to be trained very differently to the others.'

Bolger splits his horses into two groups for work purposes based on their character. 'There are many different things you have to do. For example we have two main gallops here. One is principally for

Jim Bolger – a wonderful success story

what we call the "headbangers" – not a very nice expression I admit. Those are the ones that just can't hack it with the rest of the string. It's nothing to do with a bad experience or anything, just that they are not up to training with the others. We try to keep them on an even keel all the time and it's not an easy job.'

John Francome also believes the riders have a very important part to play in how the horse feels about itself. He says: 'It is not that they lack self-esteem, it is more a question of giving them confidence. That is why to anyone who sets out training I say your biggest asset is the people dealing with the horses. The people riding them every day. The person who gives it a pat on the neck rather than the person who gives them a kick in the belly. A few need a kick in the belly but most want a pat down the neck. You get more out of them that way. You cannot put enough emphasis on the riders. When you ride a horse you should treat every horse like it's your own.'

Your best friend is the person who brings out the best in you.
Henry Ford

Sometimes a trainer has to accept that he has a loner on his hands. Sir Mark Prescott tells the tale of such a case. 'Well years ago I was sent to see a group of yearlings and when I saw one I liked I would say "That's a nice colt there" and they would say, "Well Sir Gordon (Richards) particularly liked him" so I knew that was on his way to him, and then I would see another and say "There's a lovely horse" and they would say, "Well Noel (Murless) trained the granddam" so I knew where that was going.

'We eventually got through them all and in the end there was this tiny little thing hiding under a dock leaf and they said "That's the one we are sending you by Tudor Melody" and he had clearly been thoroughly bullied by all the others and had learned to keep away from trouble. He was quite nervous to break in but he transformed physically when he was on his own as he was no longer bullied and he became a very useful sprinter called Marching On. So he was an example of one that thrived through not being in the herd.

'There are horses that never settle as well away from the herd because they derive confidence from being in it. Horses are as different as you or me. You have only to separate chickens and sheep to see that. People see them in a flock and think they are all the same but you move them into pens and start to handle them to go to a show and they are as different as you and me. Any shepherd will tell you the same. But once you get them ready for a show they become individuals.'

Dermot Weld went to great pains to deal with one case of an insecure horse.

'We had one particular filly, a three-year-old bought at the Newmarket July Sales that finished last at Nottingham and an owner bought it and sent her to me. I asked why he had bought her and he said she had a good pedigree. She was very timid but our training regime is different to the yard she had been at as we are very easy on our horses. She was a light-bodied filly that had been mentally hard trained at home. I did the exact opposite. I let her out in the paddock for a week, talked to her and gave her sugar lumps. We petted her and told her she would enjoy life here and made a fuss of her. We praised her and the stable girl went out of her way to be nice to her. The training regime was very light. The first few days she didn't eat much but we gradually coaxed her to see what she would like to eat. We gradually got her to eat. We gave her confidence in the evening by praising her. We chanced one little bit of work and she went very well. A week or two later we went to the races and she bolted up.'

Peter Makin also recalls an occasion when he had to go to great lengths to help a horse begin to feel good about itself.

'We had one particular case of a "broken" horse when he came here as a back-end two-year-old. They couldn't get him into the stalls

Peter Makin – now retired after a distinguished career

at home so they sent him to the races hoping the stalls handlers would get him in and he smashed them up and came back twice in the horse ambulance and so the owners sent him here.

'He stood in the corner for two weeks totally dejected and I had a daft girl look after him. She never stops talking anyway and she talked and talked and talked to him and built up his confidence and he thought he was King Kong. Mind you we also had him gelded and sent him to Gary Witheford and he was there for a month going through the stalls every day and his confidence built up and built up. It took two months to turn him around. A lot of tender loving care went into him all through the winter and spring.'

Dr Richard Newland is a great believer in allowing his horses time in a field. He says: 'I am very big on turnout. I train a lot of horses in the field. The grazing – they love it. And they are a lot more chilled out after doing that. Obviously I appreciate that cannot apply to two-year-old colts because they will break legs and not be safe.'

I referred in the Introduction to the story of the factory worker shouting home their winner in the betting shop and suggested that this was one of the few opportunities that person had to express a personal view. Ruth says that a horse does not get many choices in life, and by allowing it to make a decision at some point, then as an individual it has a chance to assert itself.

'It's all about turning them out and they go out every day in all weathers. The way we do it is that they all go out of the barn rather than lead them through separate paddocks. We fence some of the paddocks off to save the grass. The thing to remember is that a racehorse in training doesn't get many choices in life. It gets fed at a certain time, it goes to the gallops at a certain time and spends the rest of the day in the stable. With us they get a choice as to when they want to come in.

'In winter they go straight out into the field. If you need to keep one in for the farrier or dentist then they chase around the box at 100 miles an hour because they are looking forward to getting out and can't understand why they are not. You can't tell them they are not going out for an hour because the dentist is coming.'

In my view Ruth Carr's belief that a horse likes to be given the opportunity to make a choice gets to the heart of the matter. With humans one way of assessing emotional intelligence is the degree to which a person is prepared to accept responsibility for the choices they have made. That is why a society built around blame and litigation does not allow the individual to flourish and grow. Perhaps, in a more simplistic way, the same applies to the horse. A horse will not thrive as an individual, and fulfil its potential, until it learns to respond to new challenges and opportunities.

Cooped up in a box for 22 hours a day there is obviously a limit to the choices and opportunities open to the racehorse. Out in the paddock, with other horses, it can enjoy a variety of options and distractions – where to stand, who to hang out with and when to rest or graze.

The problem is that not every racehorse can be risked in the paddock, for reasons mentioned earlier. The task facing their handlers is to assess the individual needs of each horse. For example the horse may be a loner or perhaps be a bit of a playboy. He may be a horse that needs stimulating or, as Willie Carson said about Troy, may just be rather dull.

It is interesting that even those who suggest that it is nonsense to ascribe self-esteem or the more extreme human emotions to the racehorse have actually spoken, with great insight and understanding, about the extraordinary lengths they go to in order to build up the confidence of the more vulnerable and weaker members of their team. It's all about the members of the team being sensitive to the specific requirements of the individual – watching, listening and learning.

It may, as Peter Makin said, require nothing more than 'a daft girl who never stopped talking'.

5
Feel the Fear

Love is what we're born with. Fear is what we learn.
Marianne Williamson

A wise man once told me that there are only two things in life – fear and love.

He said that many human actions can be sourced to a fear or love-based cause. He was, of course, speaking in general terms but even so there have been many occasions when I have had reason to remind myself of his words.

For example we may go to work because we have an underlying fear of the consequences of not doing so or, conversely, because we have a passion for it. People who are the victims of abuse from a violent partner sometimes choose to stay in the relationship because they fear the prospect of being alone more than the threat of further violence.

John Lennon summed it up pretty well: 'There are two basic motivating forces: fear and love. When we are afraid we pull back from life. When we are in love, we open to all that love has to offer with passion, excitement and acceptance. We need to learn to love ourselves first, in all our glory and imperfections. If we cannot love ourselves, we cannot fully open to our ability to love others or our potential to create.'

There is no fear in love; but perfect love casts out fear …
1 John 4:18

These things are never black and white. As humans we are likely to find a variable balance in our lives between the two. Perfect love, as described in the text from the gospel of John, is something few of us can ever hope to achieve. It is fanciful outside the world of the mystic. There is, though, a rational process at work with the human. We can choose to work and interact with others, but a racehorse behaves almost entirely through instinct and, as I have illustrated elsewhere, lives 'in the moment'.

Fear manifests itself in many ways and there are two primary types of response with a horse – one conscious and the other involuntary.

In the case of the human a stressful stimulus can lead to a release of chemicals that cause rushed breathing and make the heart race. Some of the messages will lead to a conscious thought and a consequent action. Others, by contrast, produce what is called an autonomic – an involuntary – response.

In the case of a racehorse the 'fight or flight' response is entirely autonomic. It is not a result of conscious considered reasoning. Unlike humans, who have a rational brain, a racehorse will respond to fear instantly without reasoning the thing through. It responds to the threat in that moment.

The word 'fear' needs to be defined with greater clarity in relation to the experience that a horse may face.

There are degrees of fear, ranging from worry, anxiety, dread, terror, panic through to horror. Worry and anxiety are triggered by the anticipation of harm. Dread, terror and panic are linked to the threat in the immediate present, while horror is the experience of the emotion in its most extreme form. In this case the subject can be reduced to a gibbering wreck – something we can relate to humans but possibly less so to horses.

These are emotively charged words, but what we mean by fear in the context of the racehorse is probably more akin to worry, anxiety or self-preservation than the more extreme states. A horse is genetically equipped to slip into 'flight' mode. For example stress-related hormones are released in the horse as a result of sudden loud noises. Its ears move independently, so sound can arrive at each ear at slightly different times allowing it to locate the origin of the noise and respond.

A horse has the largest eyes of any land mammal and they provide a 350 degree range of vision. When both eyes are focused on an object a long way in front, the horse is using binocular vision. When it is using each eye separately this is called monocular vision. The horse's ability to escape from the predator is in proportion to the speed with which it can detect the threat. The horse potentially has the fastest response time of any domestic animal.

Luca Cumani believes that an element of fear is fundamental to the racehorse and that the horse slips into 'flight' mode when racing.

'The only weapon a horse possesses in order to satisfy its instinct for self-preservation is flight. We try and make them believe there is danger,' he says. 'That is why they race. There is no other reason for them to race. I accept that they will gallop together in the wild, but they don't put themselves through the pain barrier. You never see a horse in the wild running as fast as it does in a race. Never. If it is being chased by a cheetah, a tiger or a predator then it is running through fear. By racing horses we are playing on that response. If horses did not fear, why else would they put themselves through the barrier?

'Routine is very important for a horse. He knows he has done it many times before and is not worried or frightened. But when he has been in a horsebox overnight and stables in a strange box and surrounded by horses that he doesn't know and then gets taken into a paddock and hears a tannoy, it can be like an actor with stage fright. Their heart rate becomes elevated and they discharge adrenalin before the race. Human beings have a reason – a gold medal or fame and glory at the end. A horse does not know about fame and glory. He does not look in the *Racing Post* to read about how well he has done! A horse does not know it is a racehorse. It only knows that it is a horse. He does not know where the winning post is. The mistake we make, as humans, is to apply the intelligence of humans to a racehorse. We don't really understand the intelligence of a racehorse. Some people use derogatory terms to describe a horse that does not appear to race willingly, but it could be argued that if you were a horse you would call that an intelligent response.

A horse's intelligence is related to survival, so they are happy if they feel safe and unhappy if they feel unsafe. I do not believe that we should anthropomorphise and ascribe patterns of human behaviour to a horse. That is really as far as it goes.'

I appreciate that many followers of racing would feel deeply uncomfortable at the thought that when they watch a race they are witnessing a display of fear. It certainly never occurred to me – at least not in such stark terms. Like many others I assumed that a horse raced through training, discipline and in some cases a spirit of competitiveness. A horse raced because it wanted to, but Cumani makes a distinction between a horse galloping freely in the wild with its mates and a horse being asked to extend itself in the competitive and sometimes hard-fought setting of a race, urged along by the man on top.

Sir Mark Prescott sees himself as the custodian of a racehorse's quality of life while it is in his care. For all his talk of bull-fighting and other sports which are now frowned upon or even banned, Prescott is a deeply sensitive man who thinks long into the wee small hours about his responsibilities. He, too, believes fear has a big part to play in the day-to-day life of a racehorse.

'Fear is the horse's premier emotion because they require that to survive in the wild,' he says. 'The horse with the lower developed sense of fear or apprehension gets killed first. What man has done with progress and civilisation – and with the domestication of the horse – has been to reduce the fear factor but, in the wild, the one that survived the longest was the one which spotted the danger first. Horses are not predisposed to be competitive.

'If you had said to Spindrifter, who won 13 races for us as a two-year-old, "Would you like to go to Pontefract this afternoon?" he would say, "No thank you very much, you and George (Duffield) go, and take that Mr Waters (owner), and have a cracking day. I will stop here". If you asked Misty Halo, who won a record number of races on the Flat for a mare at that time, "Do you want to go to the races this afternoon with that nice little Elaine Mellor riding?", she would have said "No thank you, not at all. You and Elaine go and have a lovely time and I will stop here".

'No horse wants to go to the races. If anyone says to you that a horse wants to go racing then in my opinion, and I stress it is my opinion, then they have absolutely no understanding of a horse whatsoever.'

As followers of horseracing we may feel uncomfortable that a horse is being asked to race against its will. Yet, in defence of that argument, there are many occasions during the course of a day that we, as human beings, are expected to do something which is not to our liking. It is a step beyond that to say that we are motivated through fear, but then as I implied earlier, fear may be working at a subliminal level in many of our actions.

Peter Makin would not be alone in feeling troubled at the concept of horses racing through fear. He believes that generations of breeding has its part to play.

'I would not agree with that at all. Some don't want to race but in the field they take each other on galloping around. They have been bred to be competitive for generations. A horse is a flight animal, so it will sometimes run through fear, but they also have a *joie de vivre*. If I thought that a horse only ran through fear then I would not want to be training it really. You have to build up their confidence. Not every horse is competitive but the successful ones are.'

Gary Witheford belongs to the same school of thought.

'I disagree that a horse races through fear. The horse is a flight animal so it does not want to be at the back because it is going to get eaten. It wants to be in the middle of the herd. It has to have that challenge of staying alive. But if an animal fears to race then its heartbeat will go a lot faster and it will struggle to breathe. The oxygen won't get into the lungs or the brain. Good racehorses are very relaxed.

'For example Sea The Stars was so relaxed from day one that within nine minutes of starting him and getting on his back to ride him he went into his box and lay down to rest. He never had a sweat mark on him. We walked, trotted and cantered and that was the first horse John Oxx ever sent me to start.'

Irish trainer Jim Bolger believes a racehorse is happy to put itself under pressure occasionally, but not as a consequence of fear.

'I rear up to 20 colts in a paddock all together and when they begin to feel well in themselves around July time, after a couple of months of good grass, then a bunch of them gallop off and perhaps one will be six lengths behind and then put its head down and try to finish the gallop in front. The others will lob along at the tail of the bunch with not a bother in the world. He could turn out to be your best racehorse when he goes into training but his jockey has to grab hold of him and give him a slap down the shoulder. I don't think there is any element of fear in what he's doing. He knows that

John Oxx – an advocate of the gentle approach

he is being asked to put in a bit more effort and he is happy enough to do it.'

John Oxx says: 'I don't think a racehorse runs solely through fear. Why does the whip work? The thoroughbred responds, sticks his neck out and does his best. I would not attribute that to fear alone. It is running because it is bred for it. The horse is a flight animal by nature but as they become domesticated they adapt. They learn our way quickly and are not scared of people anymore. It is as if the fear has been bred out of them. They take to people very quickly and now allow themselves to be handled and to be taught the things we want to teach them. That is from breeding.'

The view that a horse is bred to be competitive is a complex one. Is it right to suggest, for example, that a horse racing against another over four miles at Smithfield in the late 12th century was exerting itself any less than the winner of last year's Derby?

Oliver Sherwood has mixed views on the subject. 'A lot of horses seem to enjoy the "battle". I have ridden horses that would die for you. They would run over a cliff for you. I understand why someone would suggest a horse races through fear, but until you find a horse that can talk to you I'm not sure anyone can answer that question. But, as a rider, you do know when a horse is trying for you. Mind you, is that through fear or a sense of commitment?'

It is not things in themselves which cause us fear, but our perception of them. Epictetus

Five-time champion jockey Willie Carson has lived with horses all his life, from his earliest days as an apprentice to his retirement from the saddle and his current role as a breeder and owner of a successful stud. He believes that the racehorse evolves through its life and adjusts in response to its handling and environment.

'I'm not sure that a horse races through fear. A thoroughbred in its early days has an element of fear because it is bred to flee in the face of danger. This is correct. But once they have been around man and have been handled the fear is not the same. I am a great believer that a horse, especially a thoroughbred, when introduced to things a few times will get used to it.

'For example if you take a horse near a railway line the first time a train comes along he will want to gallop off. But after a few weeks of the trains coming backwards and forwards he won't even lift his head up. At my stud I have a field next to me full of sheep and at the beginning of the season they want to gallop all over the place but by the end they couldn't give a shit. They will get used to almost anything.

'Having said that I have a hunter who has seen the world – horse-boxes, busy roads, fences, wagons, everything – yet at exercise he will shy at the same bin every day. Now explain that one! It's there every day but he always gives it a wide berth. There may be something from the past but I didn't have him from the early days so I

Willie Carson – a fun loving guy

don't know. I just wonder why he keeps shying away from it. He sees it and goes past it every day. Mind you he goes past it better if he is trotting. If he is walking slowly he looks at it as if something is going to jump out at him.'

Peter Scudamore agrees. 'I'm not sure that a horse races through fear. My father used to say that good horses are thick. But that is like saying a hard-working person is thick. Their instinct is to survive. No, I don't think a horse races through sheer fear. No.'

Nobody knows what a horse is thinking, but I see occasions on a daily basis when a horse appears to be racing outside its comfort zone – scrambling along, appearing to do two strides for every other horse's one. This is what happens when a horse is asked to compete outside its class. A good trainer will allow a horse to find its level, perhaps working up from lowly beginnings, while a less capable trainer will run a horse in a grade for which it is not prepared.

At school the finalists for the 100 metres sprint would probably be feeling quite nervous before the race. If Usain Bolt were asked to join them, he would be pretty relaxed about the whole thing because he knows that he will not have to exert himself unduly. But a horse is probably not as capable as a human of anticipatory feelings, such as anxiety or confidence.

The 'fear' motive may apply more to a talented racehorse than, say, to an average one. This could also be applied to humans. I remember once talking to Alan Ball, the youngest member of England's 1966 World Cup winning team who scored more than 180 league goals in a 22-year career. He left me in no doubt that fear – in his case of his father – drove him on in his formative years.

A horse that is sent to the races for a quiet run round – perhaps, for example, a two-year-old making its racecourse debut – is unlikely to be put under maximum pressure. The same may apply to a racehorse that doesn't try very hard – and, trust me, there are many of them! However, like Alan Ball, a horse that is expected to compete at the highest level has to go much further, digging deep into its resources to fend off challengers.

Michael Hills says: 'I know exactly what they are saying about fear, but through riding as long as I did I found the good ones were naturally competitive and when you asked for an effort you could feel them give everything, without needing to resort to the whip. They would just naturally do it. I'm not sure that they did that through fear.'

John Gosden says: 'If a horse is brimful of confidence then I don't think fear is a factor. All right they are creatures of flight – for example they have amazing rear vision as well as forward vision. Why do their ears go back and forth? Always listening. So if you take them back in time to when they were on the open savannah or the steppes, any movement could mean death. A predator. They don't ask any questions. They just jump and go. That is fear and adrenalin, of course. That is flight.

'But the greatest racehorses don't become unnerved. I have seen the best sprinters and they are not neurotics. They are fast, but if they blow it over the first three furlongs they are not going to see out the five or six furlongs.

'All great athletes, whether they are tennis players, racing car drivers or cricketers, have one thing in common. They have all the time in the world. They make everything look so easy, because of the rhythm of their breathing, their fitness and their sheer ability. Yes of course horses that live on their nerves can win good races, but they are hard to keep where you want them to come back time and again. The truly great athletes have that extraordinary mental composure combined with athletic ability.'

Henry Candy offers one reason why a horse may manifest signs of fear: 'The great thing you want to see in horses all the time is that they are totally relaxed and like going out on the gallops, almost sleepy and just doing the work nicely. But if a horse is far too free or running away, it's always running away from fear of something, whether it's pain in the leg or the heart or it knows it is going to bleed, you can't always see that unless you scope it all the time. And when they bleed it's rather like you or I drowning, it's the same sort of sensation.'

Any professional soldier will tell you that it is not overcoming fear but learning how to handle it that sets them apart from the rest of us. A trainer's job is to prepare the racehorse, both mentally and physically, for what lies ahead.

Sir Mark Prescott takes the military analogy further. 'If Spindrifter had been human he would have been almost emotionless. I remember seeing a famous picture of the D-Day landings, and there is an old sergeant who has obviously been into battle a million times and he's leaning on the edge of the landing craft smoking a cigarette. Around him are young men, all crouching, and each one looks terrified. You can see from his expression that he's thinking let's just get on with the fucking thing.

'That was Spindrifter. That was Misty Halo. If we're going to do it let's get on with it. Don't expect me to enjoy it. Let's just get it done. I think my best horses have been very professional. The trainer's job is to enable the horse to build up a tolerance of hard work.'

John Gosden argues along the same lines. 'In essence every horse is an individual, so it varies from one to another. It came out in the movie *Rush*, about the racing driver James Hunt. He vomited before every race, and Sir Stanley Matthews, the great footballer and the master of the dribble, was sick before every game.

'Did Sir Stanley want to play football? Yes. Did Hunt want to drive? Yes. So the point is this. They were channelling their nervous energy and being sick became part of that process. If you go into an exam as a kid there has to be a nervous build-up of energy. How else are you going to get yourself to perform at your best? Obviously, failing to control or channel your nervous energy invites panic with the inevitable consequences. So for a horse, whether its ultimate level is a Group 1 or a claimer, you don't get there by being a laid-back slob, eating crisps and watching television. You have to get into a certain zone, mentally and physically.

'I find that in the training of racehorses they are happy competing with each other as long as they are fairly matched. They find it disconcerting when they are not well matched. It's like playing tennis with someone who keeps you running round the court and barely breaking sweat themselves. For a racehorse you have to be very careful about its level of ability and not overface it because that could break its spirit.'

Fear is an emotive word and the truth is that we cannot really know what a horse feels because it cannot speak. What we can assume is that it has degrees of sensitivity. A horse may, in some cases, experience anticipatory anxiety when it goes to the races but this varies and depends on the individual and its state of wellbeing, fitness, training, ability and intelligence.

Like the old soldier at the D-Day landings the racehorse is now better equipped than ever before to cope with what lies ahead. Every living creature experiences a degree of fear at some point. The horse handler's job is to help them learn how to deal with it.

6
Do They Ever Forget?

Love is so short, forgetting is so long. Pablo Neruda

We can all recall experiences from our childhood – both good and bad – that still affect us many years later.

In an effort to relate more to this subject I thought back to a disturbing episode in my own life and reflected on the extent to which I have managed to overcome it. The one that I recall most vividly was over 50 years ago and it took place when I was at primary school in Leeds.

Perhaps because I was the son of the local vicar I was seen as a legitimate target by a gang of boys – they were a year or two older than me – and they would wait for my bus to return home and then pounce on me as I ran up the long drive through the vicarage grounds to my front door.

Many of my school hours were spent preoccupied with thoughts of finding ways to get home unscathed. It was important that I caught the 3.15 bus so I occasionally took a sneaky look at the clock which hung on the adjoining classroom wall. On this occasion my teacher Mr Soames caught me peeking, flew into a rage and told me to see him at the end of the day.

He and two other teachers then instructed me to stand in front of the clock and watch the hands turn, fully aware of the anxiety it would cause me. They waited until the clock passed 3.15 before allowing me to leave. By then I had become so upset that I had soiled myself, and had to face the ignominy and embarrassment of sharing a crowded bus for the 20-minute journey home.

How do I feel about Mr Soames now? Well clearly I have not forgotten him but I have been able to accept what happened. I mention this because it was the first awful experience I can recall.

The extent to which a racehorse can rationalise and overcome a disturbing or unhappy experience in its early days is harder to evaluate. To the untutored mind it is assumed that it would vary from horse to horse, just as an upsetting incident would affect people to different degrees. In relation to the racehorse, tests and studies seem to suggest that a horse has a very good memory.

A study by Evelyn Hanggi, co-director of the Equine Research Foundation in California, found that horses that had been tested on recognition and advanced learning abilities up to 10 years earlier were able to repeat the same tasks with a nearly perfect level of accuracy, without having to learn the skills again. As the horses had not been exposed to these tests since the time of the initial research her conclusion was that horses have a remarkable long-term memory.

Lea Lansade, a researcher in behavioural science at the National Institute for Agricultural Research (INRA) in Tours, France, says that a horse does not forget once it has learned something.

'This has both pros and cons,' she says. 'If you teach your horse something he is going to remember it for years and years – even if you have not practised it in the meantime. The downside is that if he has had a bad experience, he won't forget that either and he will resort to defence mechanisms many years later.'

Lea Lansade and Mathilde Valenchon from the INRA tested 26 horses for long-term memories. In one task the horses were taught to back up when told 'Back!' by the handler and received a reward of food when doing so. In the second task the horses had to cross an obstacle after hearing a bell ring to prevent being subjected to a puff of air.

The horses were then tested for the same task two years later, having not performed the task at any stage during the interim. To the surprise of the researchers all the horses, without exception, perfectly retained the exercise they had learned two years earlier. However when the researchers removed the reward of food, the horses tended to stop performing their tasks. In the backing-up test, the more fearful horses performed the longest after the food reward ended. In the obstacle-crossing test, it was the least sensitive horses that kept performing even when the air puff stopped.

These findings are endorsed by Dr Robert Miller, who in *Understanding The Ancient Secrets of the Horse's Mind* proposes that a horse categorises learned experiences as either something to fear, such as the puff of air in the INRA research, or something not to fear, such as the reward of food. It is the responsibility of the handler to desensitize the horse to accept certain procedures, such as farriery, dental treatment or a veterinarian examination.

This would seem to support my belief that fear, either resulting from an early experience or a race situation, can play a big part in the day-to-day life of the racehorse.

It is thought that a horse learns mainly in two ways. Non-associative learning is when the horse becomes exposed to a single stimulus, which may have originally caused fear, and becomes desensitized through training. Associative learning is when the horse learns to make associations of its own between different stimuli, for example the sound of a car driving up and the arrival of food.

Gary Witheford deals with fragile and damaged horses on a daily basis. He believes that the prime requirement for a newly-born foal is to find a leader and if that happens they are better equipped to overcome fear.

'You can repair damage quite early in life. If you go back to basics the mare has the foal, delivered on the floor, and then the mare gets up and the foal starts to get up and it goes straight to the milk bank and bonds in just minutes. The foal then looks to its mother as the leader. You see this happen if the mare dies. The foster foal then looks for another leader in the same way, perhaps me or you, or somebody that is going to feed it.

'We break that cycle normally at six months when the animal is weaned, removed with a head-collar and taught to walk beside you. If you stand in front of it he will follow you because it wants a leader. In my view it is utterly wrong that the horse has to lead by the side of you. You are the boss and once it sees you walking – say across plastic or by people with umbrellas – it will see that you are not scared and will start to do things it would not normally do within seconds, not hours, following its leader.

'Sometimes they are too far gone. I had a horse recently that would not even walk out of my barn. Never in 35 years have I seen anything like it. He had given up on himself. You could lead him or take him anywhere but as soon as you got on his back he just said no. They had tried everything – beating it, giving it a carrot or loving it but he did not want to do it. He would rather stand there and die than do anything else. He didn't even want to walk out of the pen. Sometimes he would smash himself up, whether he was up against a padded or steel gate.'

As mentioned before a horse's poor attitude may sometimes be a consequence of physical discomfort. One horse that will always be special to Witheford is Royal Mail who, in 1981 ran third to Aldaniti and Spartan Missile in the Grand National.

'Royal Mail is the horse that got me into what I am doing. He was the ultimate. He was in pain every day of his life and taught me a lot about getting a horse to loosen up. I was working for Stan Mellor when Royal Mail joined us from New Zealand in 1978 and I was the only one who ever rode him at home. He was such a sour horse when he arrived. His ears would go back at you but he was just in pain. He always had white marks where ill-fitting saddles had been used so we had a saddle designed for him. He broke his jaw at the cross-fence in the Gold Cup. They were going to put him away and I said no, let's sort this out and I rode him with just a head collar. Six weeks later he won the Whitbread Gold Cup. I invented a special bridle for him.

'He was an amazing horse. I used to take him for walks around the lanes. Like people take their dogs for a walk I take my horses for a walk. They go round the gallops and the village with me on a halter which sweetens them up. They become my friends rather than just being in the box and walking around in it like a prisoner.'

Dan Skelton, a rising star in the jump training ranks, says: 'It depends on the level of the bad experience. It's all physically linked. It may not have been fed well, for example, so it is not feeling at its best. In my opinion the mentality of the horse is all linked to physical causes.'

Foals these days are probably looked after better than they have ever been. Homebreds may be a little bit spoilt, but horses that have been prepared for the sales are generally well-mannered and know how to behave.

Trainer Henry Candy is renowned for his gentle and patient handling of horses. He says: 'I honestly think now that everyone has become so professional about producing horses that they all seem pretty happy, content and well-educated when they arrive in the yard. In the old days they may have been left to their own devices for a little bit too long, rushed or not given quite enough time to acclimatise to what would be required, and they got confused and probably a little bit frightened. A long time ago you used to get horses coming in who had been hurried a little bit, or slightly ill-treated. They were nervous and if you go back a long way you used to get horses which were regarded as savage, but that was probably only a means of self-defence.

Henry Candy – one of racing's most reflective thinkers

'But nowadays studs are fantastic, stud managers know exactly what trainers want and horses are very well-prepared. It is very rare now to get a horse come into the yard which is frightened or nasty. The whole process is working a lot better and most horses arrive pretty content, with a chance of reaching their potential.'

Having said that, Candy believes that a horse will struggle to overcome a bad early experience.

'If a horse has had a bad experience of any sort it will never forget it,' he says. 'I think horses have very good memories. I would never ask a two-year-old to jump out of the stalls more than four times unless it was unbelievably thick. That would be before their first run and I would never ask them to do it again for the rest of their lives. Whether it is instinct or memory I don't know, but they don't forget. I think they have very good memories but if a horse has had a bad experience in a certain place – on the gallops for example – it would be pretty wary of going past that place again.'

Peter Makin agrees. 'Horses are so much more professionally handled now when they go to the sales. They are almost ready to run the next week if you need them to. They are really already half-broken and that obviously makes our job much easier. You get to know the good studs. Their yearlings can be full of themselves and have a pride about them. Then from the lesser studs instead of the horse dragging the lad around the lad is dragging the horse around with its head on the ground.

'They are not born bad. They have their idiosyncrasies but if they are channelled in the right direction, all goes well and if not, and they are abused, they can turn. You get cheeky, nervous horses that take a bite at you and then frighten themselves having done it. If the lad looking after a horse knocks it about then it may eventually get more and more nervous rather than build his confidence. The people who look after the horse are all important.

'Regarding their memories I believe that it varies from individual to individual. Some are tougher than others. Some don't overcome a bad experience which is why trainers don't like a horse to get a hard race first time. If you go for broke first time the horse may think "sod it I don't like this game". You do get some tougher ones though.'

'There is no doubt that some of the horses used to be raised pretty wildly,' says John Gosden, 'and that could produce a tough horse which hadn't been handled much. The wildness was more fear and suspicion than it wanting not to please you. There is no doubt horses are handled more now at a young age which is a benefit.

'So you then get round to gaining the confidence of the young horse and that is why the whole breaking process must be about self-confidence with the horse and the handler, with the idea that you don't go after the horse but the horse must come to you, because they like the idea of what you are doing. That is how the old Native Americans used to break them in and the way Monty Roberts learnt a lot of his methods.'

This returns to Ruth Carr's belief that a horse needs to be given an opportunity to make a choice. This empowers the horse emotionally, thereby equipping it to handle difficulties later in life.

Michael Dickinson had a well-founded reputation in his training days for thinking 'outside the box'. The last time we met was at a recent Newmarket Sales and, aware of my theological background, the first thing he asked, as he sat down next to me in the dining area, was if I would explain to him the fundamental difference in beliefs between Jesus and the Prophet Muhammad! That became the subject of discussion for five minutes before he moved on to see someone else. At no stage did the subject of horseracing enter the conversation.

The story goes that someone once said to him he was half-mad. Legend has it that his reply was they were probably 'half-right'.

'Yes, karma is for real,' he told me. 'Horses mishandled at an early age are less likely to cooperate later in life. They never forget a bad experience. They need firm discipline when young or we may come up with a spoiled brat. Horses that are raced above their level of competition soon lose their confidence. That is why champions are usually more confident, but a bad attitude from a person can affect the horse.'

Jim Bolger is adamant that a horse remembers a bad experience. 'I don't think a horse ever forgets an early experience. It stays with them. If a horse gets a really bad fright it will stay with him for the rest of his life, not to mention for the few years he is in training. It is difficult to turn around if they get a really bad fright. For example a bad experience in the starting stalls can prove hard to overcome later on.'

Roger Charlton, whose career could not have made a better start when in 1990 he sent out the winners of both the English Derby and the French Derby, is less sure: 'Does a horse have a good memory? It is very hard to tell. You have to give them the respect and assume that they have. They might have been turned out with another horse in a field and I like to think they still know that paddock and that horse, but if a new horse arrives you see them looking and thinking that they haven't seen that one before. They seem to know where they are going and what is going to happen next. They want routine. The most reassuring lifestyle is one that is monotonous and routine. To go racing is a very big variable for a horse. They may appear calm and well-behaved at home but new things emerge at the track and some may not cope.'

Henrietta Knight has also seen instances of horses remembering each other after time apart. 'They never forget. Even though everything may be fine they never forget a bad experience. Yet even if horses haven't been together for two or three years you put them back in the field and they go back into their pairs. They never forget. We usually turned out between 20 and 30 horses each summer and we split them into different fields. If we put them back again a year or two later they would return to their old friends. It's like humans. They remember their friends.'

Michael Hills rode many horses on their racecourse debuts. He takes the view that the extent to which a horse can overcome a bad experience depends on the nature of it. 'It all depends on how traumatic it was for the horse. I would say if it was very traumatic then the horse may never get over it but with a change of scene some may overcome it and learn to trust people. Horses are 'first-time learners' – what you do with them first time in the race is very important. My motto was a gentle backhander if I thought I could win the race but I treated it very much like a horse's first day at school so I wanted it to have a nice experience and not overexert itself. I didn't want it to go home knackered. Later in their career the recollection of pain can still affect them but with their adrenalin up in a big race they may overcome it for a short time.'

Sir Michael Stoute has trained winners of top-class races all over the world. He makes it very clear to his jockeys that no horse of his should be given a hard race on its racecourse debut.

Michael Hills – a very gifted rider

Peter Scudamore believes a horse's first experience can be critical to the horse's future: 'Tim Forster used to say that you can teach a horse to jump well loose schooling and then the jockey gets on and ruins it. I think all creatures can lose their trust and sometimes never get it back. Or it's hard to get back. I don't think they forget. I think that a horse has a level of brainpower that enables it to survive as a horse.

'I think sometimes you can take a horse to the track and give it a hard race first time and they never enjoy racing again. I can think of horses that were better novices than ever later in their careers because they had hard races and didn't enjoy it and didn't want to do it again.'

Five-time champion jockey Willie Carson once told me that a whip does not make a horse go any faster – it just keeps it going for longer. He is uncertain whether a horse forgets a bad early experience. 'Horses don't talk so I don't know. I am not sure that anybody can answer that. What do you mean by a bad start in life? There are no savages around these days. When I was a kid there was always a savage horse but you never see one now. Horses are better looked after than they have ever been. The reason is that they are not hassled as much and do not get strapped as they did in years gone by. Today horses are so well handled from a very early age.'

Oliver Sherwood, Grand National winning trainer in 2015, has been linked with some of jump racing's best-known horses from his days with Fred Winter and then as a trainer in his own right. 'I think it is very difficult to turn a horse around if it has had a bad experience early on in life. Horses are pushed too hard now and are not always ready to take full training, especially with the intensity of modern-day training methods. If they have had a nasty experience – not necessarily in training – they become unsure of humans. Every horse and human is different. Some horses don't care about what goes on around them while another will worry and care. Like children, some take to boarding school like a duck to water while others can't hack it. They are very similar in my opinion.

'I think the earlier they are broken in or handled by humans the better, whether it is a yearling or National Hunt horse. Years ago a jumper would be broken as a three or four-year-old. That is why the French are perhaps right in breaking and handling them as yearlings and two-year-olds, and entering light training, rather than doing nothing for three years and suddenly breaking them in over a few months.'

Luca Cumani thinks there may be a more selective aspect to a horse's memory. 'Horses only have good memories for bad things, not good things. We have moved on, from treating horses as wild animals to treating them as animals which have to be cherished. More and more horses now go through the sales and so receive intense preparation and are handled for two months before the sale continuously and so they become much more amenable and less wild through being handled.'

Lesley Middlebrook, from her stud overlooking Windermere, says: 'I don't think they do forget a bad experience. So what's the worst thing that can happen? We had a foal that lost its mum at three months but she is a determined little lady. She is now named Penny Drops, and her dam Penny Cross had to have colic surgery but you can't take the foal to surgery because it is such a long process. The day her mum went off to Liverpool we had to sedate her, and then again the next day and then the day after that. We thought she needed to get out with her friends and she was absolutely fine as she was out with three other foals and two mares.

'It can be harder for a horse to overcome a bad experience with humans, for example a bad wagon loading or journey, but most times with good handling they can overcome it. Some horses have a more nervous disposition which can make them react to certain circumstances. For instance we have a family that are sensitive around their heads and can panic coming in and out of stables in case they hit their heads on the top of the door frame so we put them in boxes with high doors. Problem solved.'

John Francome believes that the horse's character is pretty well-formed from an early stage. 'I used to break in a lot of yearlings for Jeremy Tree when I was riding, and then fast forward four or five years and you would be down at the start at Newbury and they would be the same characters. I could have told you all about them. They don't change much.'

John Oxx agrees that the horse's character is moulded in those early months of its life. 'The formative years are very important. Sometimes a yearling will arrive very nervous – perhaps it has not been treated well – and it may take a little bit of time to come round. Or a two-year-old that has been broken elsewhere may have a little bit of a problem. All sorts of things can happen to yearlings growing up. Physical ailments and mental scars. They arrive with them through your gate and don't forget them.

'It is said horses are first-time learners and if they have a bad first experience it creates a bad habit and a good experience sets them on the way properly. As yearlings we need to treat them properly and break them in properly. That's where it all begins as far as we're concerned. You have to iron out the little issues they have brought with them. In the old days every stable had experienced grooms who were good at breaking horses using all the old skills, with some better than others, but a horse has to get confidence in the people around him and this is very important. If the wrong person breaks the horse in then it can have all sorts of problems and they are done for if they develop the wrong habits at that early stage. They can be with them for life.

'We have all had horses which are afraid to be touched on one side and they get a bang or something. We have one at the moment – a filly that is very funny around her right ear. You can get the bridle on but it is very difficult to get it off if it's pulled over her right ear. Where does that come from?

'With the right handling they can overcome a bad experience. But you have to build their confidence over a period of time and that is quite difficult. The horse whisperers sometimes have a trick up their sleeve which enables them to overcome these things more quickly than the more traditional ways and a little 'TLC', but what I'm saying is that they are first-time learners, they learn things quickly and bad things stay in their mind. The horse that is perfectly handled from the outset has a big start in life. They tend to have good manners and are calm.'

Sir Mark Prescott brings most of his horses along steadily. He does send out two-year-old winners, if the right horse comes along, but most of his horses have middle-distance pedigrees so their two-year-old campaigns are all about education. He also refers to the importance of a horse's first-time experience. 'If you are teaching one to swim and it goes all right the first day it will probably always go right. When you teach one at the stalls the first time you shut him in, if it all goes right it will probably always be all right. The duty of care passes from one horseman to another, so when the yearling comes to me I have a duty of care to him while he is with me. I do the best I can for him and then when he gets sold or moved on to stud or goes to jump racing that duty of care passes to the next horseman.

'But the most important duty of care is the fellow that breaks it in. Horses are now better presented than the old days but that doesn't stop the odd one coming in from a stud where it has not been well-handled, or not handled very often. A horse that has not been appropriately handled exhibits fear. He is afraid of you and starts off expecting the worst.'

There can be very obvious examples of a horse's powers of recollection. Ronnie Postlethwaite enjoyed a formidable reputation 30 or so years ago as a very successful gambler. I remember seeing his horses 'hammered' in the ring, tumbling down in price and more often than not landing the spoils. Many of his successful punts were landed on horses that were trained by his wife Charlotte.

He told me: 'I bought a horse from a guy and the horse was a bundle of nerves so I got it going and rode it out every day myself. It put weight on and I had him where I wanted him and was winning the war, put it that way. One day I was going to the gallops and the guy I bought it off saw him and said, "I see you have got him going nicely" and within 20 seconds the horse got in a muck sweat so I just took him home. So does a horse ever forget? Well this one hadn't.'

Something Dr Richard Newland said reminded me of a piece of advice I was once given by a friend. There was a problem that I really could have done without, and I told him that I was praying for it to go away. 'Why not pray instead for the fortitude and courage to cope with it,' he said.

Newland, who seldom buys an unraced young horse, can relate to that. The vast majority of his horses have had experience of racing on the Flat, in some cases racing many times, but few arrive with a totally clean bill of health.

'The majority of our horses have done a bit, been trained and run a few times,' he says. 'I am not involved in breaking horses but dealing with problems stretching back to the formative years is difficult. You end up trying to manage the problem rather than solve the problem. Some horses are very keen, some buzzy, some box walkers and the rest of it. Nervous traits probably start early in life and are difficult to resolve.'

I suppose the key is in knowing whether the horse has a problem that can be resolved or whether, as Newland says, it is one that has to be accepted and then managed. We return to one of the common themes throughout this book, which is that a horse is an individual and some cope with bad experiences better than others.

The good news is that, in the main, horses are brought up more considerately and with greater understanding than ever before. There are also the 'whisperers' like Gary Witheford and Monty Roberts who try and rebuild trust between the equine and the human.

My counselling tutor once told me, in passing as is so often the case with things that stick in your mind, that we are 'the sum total of everything we bang into'. The term used in psychoanalysis for those 'things' is introjections. For example you may be told in your formative years that Leeds United is the best football team, that boys wear blue and that all dogs bite. Over a period of time, these views and opinions build up in layers. The moment of 'self-realisation', as it is sometimes called, comes when you start to identify and remove those layers, thereby discovering your real self.

Many years ago I used to work with trainer John Jenkins, who was based those days in Epsom. At that time he sent out hundreds of winners, including winners of the Cesarewitch, Chester Cup and Triumph Hurdle. Things are quieter for him these days, but I lived near him back then and used to pop over every so often to help him select suitable races for his horses.

One evening I turned up and as I was walking through the yard I saw him leaning against the side of a box, clearly deep in thought. He didn't spot me and so I stayed out of sight to avoid distracting him. I kept popping my head round the corner to see if he had finished, and after 20 minutes or so felt I had to make an approach as the agreed time of our appointment had passed.

'Oh there you are,' he said as he heard me walking towards him. 'I'm just trying to work this fella out. Something seems to be bothering him.'

It was in those quiet moments, leaning on the stable door, that Jenkins was trying to uncover the 'real' horse – its essence, if you like. He was metaphorically peeling back those layers – all those introjections – to try and unravel what lay at its heart.

He does not know this, but I was so impressed by what I saw that a year or two later I named a horse after him. I called it Quiet Moments.

7
Oddballs, Misfits and Loners

Misfits aren't misfits among other misfits. Barry Manilow

Many of life's great achievers experienced what may best be described as unconventional upbringings, bad starts or had challenging experiences to overcome.

Albert Einstein didn't speak for the first three years of his life. Richard Branson is dyslexic. Author Stephen King's first book *Carrie*

Albert Einstein – a late starter

was rejected 30 times. Oprah Winfrey was the victim of child abuse and at the age of 14 gave birth to a baby boy who died shortly afterwards. Daniel Craig, the actor, used to sleep on park benches when he was struggling to get work. Harry Houdini used to beg for money on the streets of New York. And, famously, Vincent Van Gogh sold just one painting during his lifetime.

As discussed earlier it would be misguided to assume that that you can apply every human character trait to horses. Yet the more I have spoken with people who work alongside horses the more I have come to realise that they are capable of doing the strangest of things. Yes, most of them are happy in a herd, but whether they are champions or just plain ordinary they have their own habits and little quirks. As Paul Nicholls says: 'They are all different. They might be herd animals but I see and treat them as individuals. They are their own people.'

Sir Mark Prescott adds: 'Ninety per cent of the horses will fit into a good trainer's system fine. But there may be 10 per cent that require really individual attention. That is probably the same as a good school. The better the school the higher proportion it will suit but inevitably it won't work for a small proportion.'

One of the best horses that Dermot Weld trained was Go And Go, a son of Be My Guest, who won for him twice as a two-year-old in 1989 before spending the latter part of that season in the States, where he won the Laurel Futurity on the turf track. The following year he was back with Weld in Ireland, winning the Minstrel Stakes on his seasonal debut. Weld decided to send him back to the States for the Belmont Stakes, tackling dirt for the first time, and ridden by Michael Kinane he won by eight lengths, with Kentucky Derby winner and Preakness Stakes runner-up Unbridled well beaten back in fourth. He spent the remainder of his career with D Wayne Lukas.

'Go And Go was a horse that made me laugh,' recalls Weld. 'He was a character. When we won the Belmont Stakes with him we

Vintage Crop – had an eye for the birds

were actually based at Aqueduct and there was a lawn there where he grazed after he had done his workout. The thing is he only wanted to eat the daisies, not the grass. He used to look around until he found some.'

Vintage Crop, who was handled with consummate skill by Weld to win two Irish St Legers and in 1993 become the first overseas-trained horse to win the Melbourne Cup, could be said to have had an 'eye for the birds'.

Weld told me: 'Vintage Crop was stabled at a place called Sandown when he won the Melbourne Cup and he used to adore watching the kookaburras. He was fascinated by them, even though he had seen plenty of crows, jackdaws and swallows in the barn. He used to keep his head out of the box as he studied their flight paths and habits.'

Tony Clark, now assistant to trainer Jo Crowley, rode some of the best horses of recent times when employed by Guy Harwood at Pulborough in Sussex. Many of them were tricky customers, with rather more 'fire in the belly' than one would wish for.

'If you pulled out 20 Group 1 winners most of them would have a streak in them,' he says. 'Genetically some are like the nutty professor. It can be because they are frustrated and get hacked off because it all comes too easily to them. Or they worry themselves into a frenzy and pull out with more energy. Sadler's Wells used to sweat. He was horrible to deal with. I had a ride in the Irish 2,000 Guineas and Pat Eddery, who rode a stable companion of Sadler's Wells, told me the horse had 'gone' but he hosed in. It was just his way. Warning was a nightmare to deal with so we ran him over five furlongs to stop him getting above himself.'

One of the most extraordinary incidents I ever saw on a racetrack was back in 1988, when Ile De Chypre ejected Greville Starkey out of the saddle just as he edged clear in the final furlong of the King George V Handicap at Royal Ascot. I was working in the Press Box at the time and having filed our copy – the main races having been run – we were all relaxed and settled down to watch the last race of the day.

Ile De Chypre – star of the 'stun gun' affair

As the horses entered the final furlong Ile De Chypre suddenly swerved left and, without warning, unceremoniously deposited Starkey to the ground. It was a case of 'hold the front page' as we rushed to the bank of available landline telephones to file a frantically written account of the incident. It was later alleged that the horse had been targeted by ultrasound waves emitted from an adapted pair of binoculars, although nothing was ever proven.

The horse had talent to burn, winning the 1989 running of the Group 1 Juddmonte Stakes with Clark, who was by then his regular pilot, in the plate. 'Ile De Chypre was very tricky. I did a lot of work with him. He was nervous, horrible and sweaty. He would pull like mad and gallop through a wall. He used to cock his jaw in work and do everything in one breath. He never raced properly, always flat out and doing everything in one go. It was like putting your foot to the floor and then suddenly switching down to first gear.'

'Quirky' but 'talented' – a coupling of words I have heard on many occasions in the course of my career – would be an apt description of Ile De Chypre.

One of my favourite horses from those early years was Boldboy, a sprinter owned by Lady Beaverbrook and trained by Major Dick Hern. He raced for eight seasons in the 1970s, winning 14 Group contests including the Abernant Stakes four times. This horse became a punters' favourite over the years, often the subject of strong market support and seldom failing to deliver the goods. He was, though, rather less than straightforward to handle.

Joe Mercer rode him most of the time, but Willie Carson knew him in his later days. Five-time champion jockey Carson is now a successful breeder and proprietor of Minster Stud. In 1988 he became the only jockey in the 20th century to have ridden a horse that he bred to victory in a Classic when Minster Son stayed on gamely to beat the talented filly Diminuendo by a length in the St Leger.

'Boldboy was gelded because they couldn't get him into the stalls,' he told me. 'He was "anti-government". He thought he knew best. I think he was a bit of a savage as well. He came out with his teeth as well as his feet. He was a toughie but became more amenable after he was gelded. He used his aggression on the racetrack. You could rev him up but he was a tricky one.'

It is not only famous racehorses that have their idiosyncrasies. Ronnie Postlethwaite, who has owned horses on a small scale for many years, has witnessed some strange things. 'We used to have a horse that would stop in sight of the gallops. He would stand still for anything from two to 10 minutes. You couldn't get it to move, so we just let it stand there and have a look, and once it saw what it wanted it would carry on and that was great. Never a bother, but a lot of people would have bullied it to get on and that might have spoiled the horse.'

Cloudwalker, the horse I managed and part-owned for a number of years, was a funny old thing. The grey won a dozen races for us,

Boldboy – one of my favourite sprinters

over jumps and on the Flat, but he was a quirky customer at home. He started life with Toby Balding at Weyhill in Hampshire but it was not until he moved to Mick Lambert at Settrington, Malton that we really got to know his ways.

He was a weaver, which is a habit – generally described as a vice – that a horse acquires of swaying its head from side to side in a lateral motion as it looks out of the box. It is not known whether weaving is caused by boredom, stress or general unhappiness, but Cloudwalker – or 'Norman' as he was nicknamed by the lads – was at it most of the time.

He was kept in a row of about 10 boxes and, by pure coincidence, those in closest proximity to him were also occupied by greys. In his early days at the yard we would arrive to see his head swaying in rhythm left to right, as the others looked on through curiosity more than anything else. With the passing of time, as our visits became more frequent, we noticed his neighbours had started to pick up the habit.

It wasn't long before half a dozen of them were at it, swaying their heads like members of a boy band sashaying their way to the front of the stage for their opening song. Cloudwalker had loads of ability but like many good horses he had his quirks.

Weaving or other compulsive disorders such as crib-biting and wind-sucking are not seen in horses in feral settings. They are associated with stabling, and according to research they occur with 10 to 40 per cent of stabled horses.

There are many theories as to why a horse behaves in such a way. One suggestion is that genetically it is predisposed to forage in the wild and forge social bonds and the highly managed and ordered environment of the stable yard does not allow for this. Some horses adapt, while others do what nature tells them.

The feeding of too rich a concentrate with little access to fibre can also lead to such behaviour. The problem is exacerbated if the habit leads to the release of tensions and consequent repetition. Another theory is that the stabled horse becomes frustrated due to little opportunity for choice. One example is that they have no control of feed times, something with which Ruth Carr will concur.

I managed another horse, also trained by Toby Balding, named Faithful Don. He proved a consistent performer both on the Flat and over jumps until it was decided to castrate him with a view to sending him over fences. Thereafter his form deteriorated, to such an extent that on more than one occasion he proved reluctant to race. At Chepstow back on the Flat one day it was as if he was auditioning for that old Hamlet cigar advertisement, planting himself in the stalls as the gates opened.

Faithful Don was probably quite an intelligent horse, having decided that racing was not for him. Sabin Du Loir, by contrast, proved top class on the track but was also evidently a horse blessed with great insight.

Peter Scudamore, who won the jump jockeys' championship eight times, rode some of the greatest horses of recent years. His 13 Cheltenham Festival victories included two Champion Hurdles and a Queen Mother Champion Chase, but Sabin Du Loir is the horse that he rates as good as any of them. Trainer Martin Pipe also held him in great affection – 'just about my favourite horse', he said – about the horse that beat the great Desert Orchid three times and Dawn Run among his total of 21 victories.

Scudamore says: 'I'll tell you what I did see once. Sabin Du Loir was one of the best horses I ever rode and if I said to him we were going to gallop through that brick wall he would say "where is it and how high?" I once turned him out and there was a foal nearby and he pulled away from me and went to attack the foal and tried to kill it. He was one of the kindest horses I ever knew but he went at it with his mouth wide open. The foal virtually fainted. I pulled Sabin away and put him back in the stable. I was completely shocked. I would have put my children in there with him. It turned out the foal was a wrong 'un. The vet came to look at it and it was a shaker with a nervous disorder and had to be put down. Sabin knew. It's like crows. They will kill the weak one.'

Henrietta Knight was renowned for her patience in the handling of her horses. Triple Gold Cup winner Best Mate ran just 22 times for his 14 successes, but one of the most difficult horses she ever had through her hands was Impek. The horse started his life with Francois Doumen in France and by the time his career ended he was the winner of 11 races including four at Grade 2 level.

'Impek was a tricky one,' said Knight. 'He tried us more than any other horse we ever had. When he arrived from France we struggled to get him to move anywhere. He would go past the yard gate and then try to come straight back in again. He went backwards everywhere and we always had someone at the start for a race otherwise he would plant himself. It was more nerves than anything else. He had done well in France before we had him but had won his bumper races out of starting stalls. He had huge ability but everything had to be right for him. We used to take him up to Mick Channon's gallops and if we were able to unbox him near the bottom of the all-weather, we could get him there once but struggle to get him there a second time. You had to lead him everywhere but once you got him going he was brilliant.'

Sir Mark Prescott recalls an experiment he once conducted on Misty Halo who, with 21 wins from 42 starts, achieved a post-war record for a mare.

'We tried some interesting animal psychology with Misty Halo,' he recalls. 'She was always reluctant to walk up the yard and into the box to go racing. We used to have to chase her all the way so, towards the end of her career, I conducted an experiment to find out how she knew she was going racing, because she used to walk up the yard plenty of other times without any bother at all.

'So one day we put a bridle on her and led her up the horse ramp and it all went fine. We then put knee boots on her, led her up the yard and she was again fine because she often had knee boots on to go trotting. We then also put bandages on her back and front and because she often had bandages on she was good again. We then put a roller on and she was still fine. We then put her back into her box and put a tail bandage on, walked her out and she stopped immediately – she never had a tail bandage on unless she was going racing.

'That gave us the answer we were looking for. If that doesn't interest you then nothing will!'

Bloodstock agent and equine complementary therapist Linda Sadler has ridden out for many of Newmarket's top trainers in her time. They include Sir Henry Cecil, Luca Cumani and Sir Michael Stoute.

'I tended to get all the difficult fillies when I was working for one particular trainer. There was one filly, a grey, who was rather neurotic. I was probably the only person she didn't injure. She came over from Italy and was nervous when she arrived. She was a bad weaver, bouncing from foot to foot and we struggled to even get a saddle on her. When she was out she wouldn't go on the gallops and when she did eventually get on them she would pull like a train, but she was very good. She reared over backwards on one lad, broke one girl's finger and another girl's thumb, but I rode her for a year and we managed to survive all the exercises without injury and got her to win a Listed race at Ascot and second in a Group 3 in Italy. She has become a highly successful broodmare, breeding a French 1,000 Guineas winner, who also bred the same. Without the patience and understanding of her trainer, she would not have achieved this success.'

What is the secret to her success with fillies? She says: 'I have always been interested in natural healing and I knew that when you stroked a horse it isn't just comforting. It releases biochemicals in the skin which relax the horse. Massage and stroking is more effective than people would believe, and I mean a stroke not a little pat. I did a lot of stroking and talking. That also helps them to breathe properly and relax. When riding, especially on a strong puller, the horse tends to relax if you talk to it as it is listening to you.'

Frankel has been described by many as the greatest racehorse they have ever seen. He is one of the few racehorses of recent times – perhaps the only one since Red Rum and Desert Orchid – to become well-known outside racing's close-knit community. Frankel wasn't easy to handle, and nor were his full-brother Noble Mission and half-brother Bullet Train. He was a colt with explosive power but there was an edge to him which, in other hands, could so easily have sent him on the wrong path.

Kind – dam of the great Frankel

Frankel is now a household name, but rather less is known about his dam Kind, who was by Danehill out of a Rainbow Quest mare called Rainbow Lake.

Roger Charlton, who trains at one of racing's finest yards at Beckhampton, knew her better than most. 'I trained Kind, who was a supreme looking individual and in appearance very much like her sire Danehill, who had also been here at Beckhampton. From day one she had something extra in terms of physique. She was a very good mover, very powerful but became rather impatient and keen and difficult at the stalls. Someone always had to be down at the start with her to lead her in. I thought she had the ability to become a Guineas filly as she had a pedigree packed with stamina and a little bit of speed thrown in but she wouldn't relax.

'It was to Sir Henry Cecil's great credit that he contained Frankel. He had no intention of turning that horse into a July Cup winner which, let's face it, he could have won on his head. Henry took the difficult route rather than the easy one and clearly some of Kind's characteristics came out in Frankel. In hindsight they would have been obvious candidates for a hood. This was the case with Frankel's full brother Noble Mission, who wore a hood on all but two of his 21 starts.'

In the States, but very seldom in the UK, all horses are accompanied to the start by a pony. At home dogs, sheep, goats and even chickens have been employed as companions for horses. The great US champion Seabiscuit had an assortment of companions, which included a horse named Pumpkin, a dog named Pocatell and a spider monkey, who answered to the name Jo-Jo. The 1990 Kentucky Derby winner Unbridled had an equine companion named Mustard. The companion pony may assist the thoroughbred in training and on the day of the race, when a leather strap connects it to the horse's bridle. Called 'escort horses' the pony has to have a calm disposition.

Frankel – brilliantly handled by the late Sir Henry Cecil

Roger Charlton says: 'I think the system of using a pony to lead horses down in the US and Hong Kong works very well. We had a horse called Dundonnell who was very highly strung. We used a pony with him on the gallops and he loved it. It also worked very well for him in the Breeders' Cup, when we also fitted him with ear plugs, which we removed at the start. A pony gives the horse a friendly face to look at and added confidence. Horses have ears that rotate 180 degrees. They swivel to listen out for danger and have a greater range of hearing than us. So a hood helps them blank out the noise and hustle and bustle of the races.'

In 2008 Derby winner New Approach was accompanied to the start by a pony. 'The pony was only used as an anchor,' says his trainer Jim Bolger. 'It was not needed from a psychological point of view. Actually he was a very independent horse and didn't need company. It was on his third run as a two-year-old that Kevin Manning had difficulty in pulling him up at the seven-furlong start so we took no chances after that. I always had a good rider on the pony and there was no way he was going to let New Approach run away.'

Bolger faced a wayward talent with Condessa, winner of the Yorkshire Oaks after being bought as a yearling at Goffs for just £13,000. The owner had given Bolger £20,000 to buy a horse, but he could not find another one so gave the rest of the money back. It all ended up quite well, though, as Condessa was later sold for £350,000.

'If you see any photographs of Condessa she always had a "breaking bit" on her because she would hang left and right in her races. The strange thing was that despite being light-framed she took a lot of work to get fit. When she won the Yorkshire Oaks I had given her a run on the Saturday before. It was the same when she won the Musidora Stakes; she had won the Lingfield Oaks Trial the previous weekend. Her best runs came less than a week after her previous race. She was my first Group 1 winner and Declan Gillespie did a wonderful job with her.'

John Gosden has the rare distinction of having trained at the top level in the States and the UK. Two of his best performers are Benny The Dip, winner of the 1997 Derby, and before that Bates Motel, winner of three Grade 1 stakes races in 1983 including the Santa Anita Handicap.

'Benny The Dip was "on the edge". He was a Silver Hawk and could get very sweaty and lose it quite quickly. He was neurotic and could have gone the wrong way and been too free. He would want to finish it all in six furlongs.

'Bates Motel was a complete thug. If he had been human he would have been in the wrong gang and spent most of his life behind bars. He was a total delinquent in his attitude and was huge and strong. It took a few runs before he broke his maiden. All he wanted to do was lay on horses and crash into the rails, but if you tried to bully him he would react against you. In the end I managed to exercise some cunning and we kept him very wide of horses, so he used to sweep around the outside and he became a champion. If a rival tried to get clever and sneak up the inside he would just want to wipe him out. He didn't want to go forward he just wanted to thump them.'

How did Gosden deal with such an attitude?

'It was pretty obvious to me that he needed educating into a style of racing where he was allowed to come from a long way back and sweep wide of the field. We had to avoid him getting into the pack otherwise he would try and beat them up. In one of his last races he and a horse called Slew O'Gold went along the outside fence at Belmont and forgot about a horse called Highland Blade, who won the race, and they ended up fighting for second and third virtually on the slope on the outside of the track leading to the tunnel under the grandstand.

'So there you have it. Benny The Dip was a neurotic and Bates Motel was a thug.'

Ruth Carr, who trains about 40 horses in North Yorkshire, would be the first to admit that she operates at a more modest level. Yet her record with horses acquired from other yards stands the closest inspection, and she is well-respected in an industry in which people can be very quick to judge.

Carr turns her horses out together in the paddock for a few hours every day, so she can watch and assess their individual characters and patterns of behaviour from her kitchen window, allowing her to talk with great insight about every horse in the yard, noting their character traits, habits and moods. As stated she likes to allow her horses the freedom to be with other horses in a paddock, offering the chance to exercise a personal judgement. They may, for example, choose to stand alone in the corner. Or they may try to be the first out of the gate.

'We have a horse called Orpsie Boy who is unbelievably grumpy' she tells me. 'He likes to rip his rugs into shreds, which is really annoying. We put a scruffy old cheap one on top of the good one and hope that protects the good one. He pulls faces too, but we've had him a long time and he's won races so we just think that's grumpy Orpsie.

'It's odd, though, because he can't stand the clippers but is as good as gold with the dentist. The strange thing is that he's not grumpy in the field. It's only in his stable. Despite that, when it's time to come in from the field he is one of the first at the gate. That is the place in his life where he gets a choice. He chooses to come in early whereas most of my others prefer to come in later. You get to know them and become quite attached to their little ways. "Grumpy" Orpsie is always ready for his dinner. Another horse that I once had named Head Space used to knock the scoop of feed as you try and put it into his bowl, which was annoying as it can fall into the bedding.

'I suppose some may say that I lack ambition not to want to train 100 horses, but this way I know them all and their traits. For example I always knew that something was bothering Head Space if he didn't knock the feed out of my hand. Imperial Djay liked to go out in a field but he didn't want to mix in. He liked to stand in a certain place. He was a strange customer. He really did create if you didn't let him out. I thought originally that he wasn't enjoying himself so I put him in a different paddock but he escaped and took himself back to the one where he wasn't enjoying himself.

'We had another horse called Al Muheer. He always wanted something in his mouth in the lunge ring if he could get away with it. I lunge them all loose and if my mobile rang and I looked away, he would pick up the lunge whip in his teeth and start to shake it around. If you saw him in the field he would often be carrying a stick with him. I really don't know why.'

One of the best horses Oliver Sherwood trained was Large Action, winner of 15 races including nine at Graded level.

'Large Action couldn't be bothered with anything,' he says. 'On an open day he would hide in the corner of his box. He could not be bothered with people. He went through his routine and was a joy because I didn't have to train him mentally.'

Dr Richard Newland says the same about his 2014 Grand National winner Pineau De Re. 'Pineau De Re is more of a leader but also a loner as well. He does not rely on being around other horses. Some horses have to be with company and become upset if they are on their own. Pineau doesn't seem to bother.'

Kauto Star, the five-time winner of the King George VI Chase and the only horse to regain the Cheltenham Gold Cup, had his own way of doing things. Dan Skelton knew him well during his time with the horse's trainer Paul Nicholls.

'Kauto Star had a strange eating habit. He used to take a mouthful of food and then go to the water bowl for some water. He used to keep alternating between a mouthful of food and a sip of water. That is just how he was. He ate every meal of his life that way.

'When we first got Ptit Zig he wouldn't come out of his box when it rained. Yet in the wild it would have rained on him a lot. Tidal Bay was just plain angry! He just didn't want to play a role with humans. Once you got on him he used to love the competitive element of racing but he didn't like being brushed. Perhaps something happened that made him that way. He used to bite people even though they were being nice to him. He did get better though.'

David Pipe remembers his father Martin training an 'oddball' back in the 1990s. Skipping Tim joined the yard as a 10-year-old in 1989 and won a further 26 races, racing for the last time as a 15-year-old at Exeter in May, 1994. This was a remarkable transformation for a horse that before joining the yard had won a lowly selling handicap chase at a Newton Abbot meeting in July.

'Skipping Tim was very keen to ride at home and had to go down to the gallops by himself. If he had gone down with other horses it would have blown his brains and he would have injured himself or his jockey. He didn't want to be touched in the stable and liked to be left alone. There was one girl that looked after him who he "half" trusted. She didn't treat him like a normal horse. She would basically "flick" him over rather than use a proper brush because of his aversion to being touched. Something must have happened to him as a younger horse but having acquired him at 10 we were not going to change him at that age but we learnt what he liked and he went on to win all those races.

'Pridwell was another that father turned around. He had run just three times on the Flat for Roger Charlton and Dad bought him for just 8,500gns at the Newmarket Sales back in 1993. He went on to win 14 races over hurdles including a Grade 1 at Aintree, beating Istabraq by a head. We got him so cheap because we were the only idiots at the sales who didn't know you couldn't get the horse on the gallops.'

Carrie Ann was the horse that first did the business for Martin Pipe, landing a massive touch at Haydock in 1980. She had her ways though. David says:

'Father went out to feed Carrie Ann in the field one winter and it was so cold that he had three coats on. She went for him, picked him up around his back, gave him a shaking and then chucked him to the ground.'

Peter Makin is one of the most well-respected members of the training profession. Since first taking out a licence in 1967 he has sent out the winners of many of the calendar's top races, including the King's Stand Stakes twice, the Queen Mary Stakes and numerous top handicaps.

His best-known horse is top sprinter Elbio, dual winner of the King's Stand Stakes at Royal Ascot. It is, though, another horse that keeps him entertained at the moment.

'Old Morache Music is an extraordinary horse' he says. 'He makes me laugh most mornings. We always turn them straight out when they come back into the yard from work – we have a big pen that was once a tennis court and is now full of sand – and we use it for lunging and turning horses out. Morache Music won't go back into his box until he's gone out to the pen, had a roll and a kick and then he comes in happy. If he isn't allowed to go into the pen he will just plant himself or stands up on his hind legs. He is too clever to fall over but knows exactly what he is doing. He has definitely become more eccentric as he's got older.'

Michael Hills, who rode winners of the Derby, Ascot Gold Cup, Coronation Stakes twice and many other top races, remembers Champion Stakes winner Storming Home.

'Storming Home had tremendous ability but was always looking round and not concentrating,' he recalls. 'He would jump at a piece of grass so we put blinkers on him but when we did that he got down on the ground and tried to scrape them off. That is why he wore cheekpieces and he was the first horse to win a Group 1 with them on. He gave so much to win the Champion Stakes and then he went to America and they put the blinkers on. He threw Gary Stevens off when he was in the States. I don't know what was going on inside his head. I rode him in the Japan Cup and he was a bit of a lad, and as we came out of the tunnel there were 100,000 people in front of us and a row of ponies with flags and when he saw them he got up on his hind legs and walked straight towards them. He was a man's horse.'

One of the strangest and, I think we can assume, one of the most intelligent horses that Hills ever had anything to do with was Red Clubs, winner of the Group 1 Betfred Sprint Cup at Haydock in 2007.

'My father Barry, who trained him, had three barns with 50 horses in each barn and Red Clubs was in the bottom barn and somehow one night he managed to get out. How he got out I don't know because the boxes had bars you pulled down to close the doors. Anyway he got out and walked round the bottom barn and then into the second barn, so he managed to get past 100 horses.

'He then got into Dad's garden, which had a life-size deer made out of wire. He jumped on that but having derived little satisfaction gave it a good kicking and returned to the top barn to find his mate, who he used to work with all the time. In the morning when the staff went to feed them he was stood next to his mate's box nuzzling him. The head lad said they looked like a couple of gay boys. Then just a few days later, can you believe, he won the Group 1 Betfred Sprint Cup at Haydock.'

Idiosyncratic or extrovert behaviour is, in any living creature, an example of freedom of expression but it is less likely to manifest itself as fully in a strictly regimented or structured environment. In fact the suppression of it could lead to frustration and anxiety.

I have been lucky enough to spend a fair amount of time with actors and performers over the years. In the majority of cases they

Red Clubs – the one that got away

can, let's say, be difficult. I have seen tantrums, anger, petulance and, on occasions, downright spitefulness but then that is balanced out by performances that can, at times, border on the genius. That is the price you have to pay if you want to be part of the good times. In my experience people who are touched by talent do not, in the main, have an evenly distributed deck.

As with so much in the management and training of a racehorse it is all a question of balance. Handlers vary in their approach – based to a great extent on the type of horse they are dealing with. There may be traditional beliefs in how to manage a racehorse, but there are no hard and fast rules. It is all about giving each horse the attention it requires to thrive as an individual and, consequently, to fulfil its potential on the track.

Yet there is an endless fascination in observing these character traits and if that means allowing a horse an occasional quirk or foible, then so be it. The knack is to know where to draw the line.

8

The Leader of the Pack

*A man who wants to lead the orchestra must turn
his back on the crowd.* Max Lucado

One of my few regrets in racing is that my interest started a little too late to see the horse that is generally acknowledged as being the greatest of recent times.

Arkle ended his career with a *Timeform* rating of 212 – the highest mark ever awarded to a chaser by that well-respected organisation. To give an idea of how that compares with the modern era, Sprinter Sacre was rated on 192 at his peak and Kauto Star attained a mark of 191.

Arkle won 27 of his 35 races and triumphed in three consecutive Gold Cups (1964, 1965 and 1966). Yet, unlike the top horses these days, he also contested handicaps, always under crippling burdens, notably winning the 1964 Irish Grand National under 12st, two stones more than his nearest rival, and the 1964 and 1965 Hennessy Gold Cups, both times under 12st 7lb. He surpassed even those efforts when conceding 16lb to Mill House in the Gallaher Gold Cup, breaking the course record in the process – it subsequently stood for over 40 years – but his best performance came in defeat when he failed by just half a length to concede 35lb to subsequent Gold Cup runner-up Stalbridge Colonist, with 1969 Gold Cup winner What A Myth back in third.

To be a great champion you need to have a great adversary, and that came in the form of Mill House. The 18-hands giant, known by many as 'The Big Horse', had won the 1963 Gold Cup and left his trainer Fulke Walwyn speechless when Arkle beat him a year later by five lengths: 'The most shattering moment in my husband's career. He thought Mill House was unbeatable,' recalled his wife Cath years later. Peter O'Sullevan's commentary is etched forever into the grainy black and white film footage as Arkle takes the lead from the mighty Mill House: 'This is the champion, this is the best we've seen for a long while … I'll let the crowd take over as you hear the reception that this great horse is receiving, English joining Irish and giving him an immensely well-deserved ovation.'

'The Arkle story is much much more than a racing story,' says author and journalist Brough Scott. 'It's to do with a nation having a yearning for something – something they can really believe in. Like all great events – like great masterpieces – the more you look at them the greater they become.'

'He was different, better than any horse before or since,' says author and journalist Alastair Down. 'He had a swagger to him, head in the air taking everything in, the look of eagles with a turn of foot you

Arkle – one of the greats

couldn't believe possible in a staying chaser. Arkle played with them in the Gallaher Gold Cup, winning by a long way. He was the first media superstar of the time and he moved us into the modern age. He was a phenomenon but he is also our pride, joy and enduring treasure still ...'

Sean Magee, author of *Arkle: The Story of the World's Greatest Steeplechaser*, says: 'His huge advantage in life was that nobody hurried him. Nobody expected a lot of him earlier on.' Jim Dreaper, son of Arkle's trainer Tom, says: 'My father had the most incredible patience with horses. He totally ignored their age. He allowed a horse to say when he was ready, rather than name a day six months in advance. That was his secret.'

Said, jokingly, to have drunk a couple of pints of Guinness a day – the company offered him a lifetime's supply – Arkle was the recipient of fan mail, sometimes simply addressed to 'Himself, Ireland'.

Arkle showed mental fortitude on any number of occasions – certainly when recovering from what had looked a calamitous error at an early fence in the 1966 Gold Cup and the many times he carried those mighty weights in handicaps. Yet his tenacity was accompanied by an exceptional talent, propelling him to record-breaking achievements, some of them unlikely to be surpassed.

Arkle was a truly great horse – certainly the best chaser of recent times – but to what extent does it follow that a top-class horse has a dominant or even strong character?

The term 'alpha' is often used to describe the dominant member of the herd. Alpha animals are usually more aggressive, protective and bossy. They tend to require more careful handling than the others. There is obviously a difference between the natural herd, where the mix changes in accordance with nature, and the domestic herd, or paddock scenario, which is directed by humans.

Peter Scudamore is far from sure that the best racehorses are necessarily dominant characters. 'Boss mares and alpha males – I don't know if the leader of the pack is the better racehorse. Maybe it is but I have seen the outcast of the pack be a good horse.'

Michael Dickinson doubts that there is necessarily a link between the character of the horse and its ability. 'When horses are yearlings they usually run around big fields in groups and people make the claim three years later that "I always knew he was going to be the best because he always ran the fastest in the field ahead of the group". I'm sure this is true on some occasions but there must be some instances when their memory isn't quite as good as they thought it was.'

Trainers will talk of alpha horses, especially in relation to their tenacity, and Jim Bolger produces them tougher than most. Dawn Approach was one of his best, starting his career in the first race of the season as a two-year-old at the Curragh in March, 2012, before winning a further five races that season culminating in the prestigious Dubai Dewhurst Stakes at Newmarket in October. He started his three-year-old campaign with an imperious five-length success in the 2,000 Guineas before finishing last in the Derby, not staying the mile and a half after refusing to settle. He returned just 17 days later, dropping back to a mile, and beat Toronado by a short head in the St James's Palace Stakes at Royal Ascot.

'I could not say that the good colts I had were necessarily alpha types,' says Jim Bolger. 'I am told that Dawn Approach is very good at his job of covering mares – he likes them and is keen to get on with it. Yet he never took any interest in females around the place when he was with us so I am happy to learn that he has settled into his new job. But I would never have regarded him as the sort of colt that couldn't wait to get his first mare. Perhaps having been 'blooded' with the first one he was keen to get a second. He didn't show any alpha signs here at all but he had a marvellous constitution, a great mentality and a good mind about him.'

St Jovite was a world champion and was one of the best winners of the King George VI and Queen Elizabeth Diamond Stakes that I have seen. The 1992 running was not a vintage renewal, but St Jovite did it the hard way, making all the running and powering away to beat Coronation Cup winner Saddlers' Hall by six lengths.

St Jovite was also trained by Bolger. 'St Jovite was positive in the sense he knew what his job was and wanted to get on with it, in a serious but not an overexuberant way. He was good at conserving energy through a race. He was lazy at home and definitely didn't show any alpha signs. Fillies didn't seem to bother him; he behaved like a gelding. Even though he put on those good displays I didn't get the chance to test his mettle with regard to longevity. I am still waiting to get one better than him!'

New Approach, winner of the Derby and the English and Irish Champion Stakes, was another 'toughie' who thrived in his care.

St Jovite – a world-class performer

'He was the one that amazed me the most. He always gave his best and was very very tough. His last run was his best, when he broke the track record by nearly a second, and the horse he beat by six lengths was Twice Over, who came back to win the Champion Stakes the following two years. He did everything to get himself beaten in the Derby but put his head down and ran to the line. Unfortunately he pulled a muscle in his hip before the Irish Derby and then his run in the Juddmonte put him right for the two Champion Stakes. I think he would have been a better four-year-old but he was not the easiest horse to train so I was not spending too much time trying to persuade Sheikh Mohammed to keep him for another year! He has become such a success at stud that I don't have any regrets.'

Mental toughness, though hard to define, is something the trainers of top horses talk about. It's the same in any sport. My tennis coach once told me that that there is probably not a great deal of difference in the technique and ability of the world's top dozen tennis players. At that level it's mental toughness, commitment and focus that makes the champion.

John Oxx's Sea The Stars was one of the toughest and most versatile horses of the last 10 years, achieving the remarkable feat of winning a Group 1 race every month of his three-year-old career from May to October inclusive. Those victories included the 2,000 Guineas and the Derby. A few years earlier Oxx had trained Azamour, whose four Group 1 victories included the St James's Palace Stakes and the following year's Prince of Wales's Stakes.

'I have found that the best horses have a mental toughness,' says Oxx. 'That is the distinguishing factor between the really good ones and the top horses. There are many talented horses but they fall short in terms of consistency. It's like footballers and athletes – it's the mental toughness which puts them apart. I trained Sea The Stars and Azamour in similar ways. They always worked harder than the rest because they thrived on it. Azamour was a dominant male. If he had been in the wild he would have killed every other stallion and been the last one standing.

'In the natural state they follow the leader. I think a lot of the best horses have been dominant types. Azamour and Sea The Stars would stand out from the pack as having a dominant mentality. I remember Vincent O'Brien saying years ago that the dominant type of horse made the best stallion. I think a lot of those really good horses do stand out in the crowd.'

By contrast Sinndar, who won the 2000 Derby, was more laid-back. 'Sinndar was quiet,' says Oxx. 'My grandmother could have ridden him, but you had to watch him in the second half of the year when the autumn came round. He got more aggressive then. He had a bombproof temperament and always had something left in the tank.'

It is said that a tough mare will beat a tough colt, and John Oxx has handled two of the best mares of recent times in Ridgewood Pearl and Timarida. Ridgewood Pearl won six of her eight starts, easily winning the Irish 1,000 Guineas before taking the Coronation Stakes, and ended her career with a two-length victory in the Breeders' Cup Mile. Timarida was kept very busy, running eight times as a three-year-old and then seven times at four, winning at the highest level in Ireland, Germany and the USA.

'Ridgewood Pearl was tough, tough, tough. She was like a colt and never disappointed in her work. She never worked badly. Timarida won 10 races including the Beverly D. Stakes, the Champion Stakes, the Matron and the Prix de l'Opera.'

John Gosden has noted the mental toughness of fillies in their home environment.

'Let's talk about starting stalls,' he says. 'If a horse has genuine claustrophobia and panics in there then that is a severe problem which needs to be dealt with in a very sensitive manner. But if a colt is being ignorant and has been in twice running no problem and suddenly decides that he doesn't want to, you can literally lift him in and he will say "OK".

'But a filly will not. If she decides she doesn't want to go in there she would prefer to lay down and die in front of the stalls rather than go in. Funnily enough the mental strength of most fillies, productive and positive as well as negative and destructive, is stronger than in a lot of males. This is something you learn down the years, which is why a great race filly can have that ability to be better than the colts. So it is not about brute strength. It is about athleticism and mental focus. We spend a lot of time training the bodies but it's the mind which is the ultimate fascination.'

Michael Hills notes that the mare can often be in charge. 'In a herd the dominant one is often the female rather than the stallion. The boss mare takes charge and leads them everywhere. But in racing when we are trying to tunnel their vision and regiment them it takes that away from them for a while. They are more impressionable when they are young.'

Peter Makin has also seen plenty of strong-willed females in his time. 'Horses are not really too dissimilar from dogs. They like to please and you get alpha males with dogs. Like humans they stand out a mile. They are herd animals. There is always a stallion and a matriarch mare. It's the same with elephants. You get a matriarch in a herd of elephants.

'I turned three horses out the other day for a winter break – one gelding and two fillies – and within ten minutes one of the fillies was top dog. She sorted the other two out. They went their own way and started grazing. The gelding was a bumptious sort of fellow and came up thinking he was King Kong but she belted him and put him in his place. He then went up to the other filly thinking she would be easier and she quickly put him in his place as well. In the end he was the underdog.

'It's amazing how things have changed,' he adds. 'Years ago they were like fighting cocks kept in the dark. It was a terrible way to keep them. They are herd animals and even now I don't think horses in training have enough freedom. It's lovely if you can turn them out in the paddock for a few hours every day or in the sandpit for a roll. You can put colts into the horse pens these days if only for half an hour. It gives them a change of scenery and some fresh air. They can have a jump and kick and a roll and it keeps their mind right.'

Lesley Middlebrook believes it is possible to spot natural leaders on the stud from an early age. She says: 'If you put a group of youngsters together and they have been brought up in a field together and you wean them together there will be one which will be dominant. They will have put themselves into that kind of order. But if you introduce a foal, say from the December Sales, they alienate it. It can take a while before they are accepted into the herd and sometimes it can be better to introduce them to one foal in a separate paddock for a while so that they can gain confidence with a new friend. You couldn't put your hand on your heart and say that you would know which is the alpha but sometimes it can be in their pedigrees. Certain lines behave as you would expect. Whether it makes a difference to how they perform on the track is debatable. Possibly the best horses are not necessarily Alphas.'

Newmarket trainer Alan Bailey believes there is hierarchy from the outset. 'It is the same as cattle and chickens. There is a pecking order. They will go into a shed and the main one is the last to go in. I let fillies out for a couple of hours in the afternoon. I am a great believer in turning horses out here. Even unraced two-year-olds every day. There is always a top dog and a ranking down to the bottom. I never turn out an odd number because of bullying. Six horses in three pairs. We do have the odd one which is not a good mixer.'

Alan Bailey – an underrated handler

Michael Dickinson was turning out his horses in fields years ago, and it was a practice he maintained when he moved to train in the States. He does not, though, believe that the pecking order bore any relation to the horse's subsequent ability.

'When we trained steeplechase horses in the UK we used to turn them out for eight weeks in the summer,' he says. 'We had 10 fields and put four horses in each field but they were never happy. They always wanted to be in the next field whichever field you put them in. They were always the wrong side of the gate! As a result in our second year at Harewood we opened all the gates, put all the 40 horses in together and let them roam the whole farm. This not only resulted in much happier horses they were also healthier and fitter.

I spent many hours out there watching their behaviour. Unlike the people looking at yearlings I knew at the time which were the best horses and the bravest horses and their place in the pecking order bore absolutely no relation to their ability or courage. In fact sometimes it was almost the opposite. We had two horses who, when it came to racing, weren't as tough as they might have been but those two were nearly always ahead of the group and appeared to be in command. However, it turned out they were like the schoolyard bully, brave when he is in charge but not so brave when he is taken on. We had one horse who was always way behind the whole group and never really joined in but on a racecourse he won six races on the trot and was courageous and gave it all.

'Horses aren't designed to be in a stable for 23 hours a day. We think it is very important that they are turned out not just for 10 minutes in a small field with mud and weeds but for four hours in a larger paddock with fresh green grass. At Tapeta Farm we have over 50 acres for grazing. Cetewayo had been in training with four trainers, myself included, and his performances were not good. However once we moved to Tapeta Farm we had the facilities to turn him out for several hours a day and he suddenly became a new horse and went from a claiming horse to winning over $1 million and two Grade 1 races. Turning your horse out, preferably with a friend, is the best thing you can do for the horse's mind.'

When John Gosden worked for Vincent O'Brien he got to know Alleged pretty well. Alleged was one of the few horses to win the Prix de l'Arc de Triomphe in successive years, taking the race in 1977 and 1978, but he had an edge to him and was not one to cross.

'We have all come across horses that have a slightly aggressive side to their nature like people but that is rare,' says Gosden. 'You used to have old horses turn savage. I have seen some fillies who are quite keen to kick you and there are stallions that turn savage. I find the quieter and easier you are around them then 99 per cent are very affectionate really. Alleged was a horse I knew when I was young. He could turn on you pretty quickly. He knew where to go for you and he took some handling as a stallion later on. It's a tiny percentage though.'

Dan Skelton has also witnessed displays of both strong character and affection in the paddocks. 'In my experience if you turn them out in a field the "bolshie" one is either the best or a thug. Twist Magic would stand by himself in the corner. You had to take the gentle approach with him. Some days he would be fine but you didn't try and fight him. Sanctuaire relished taking you on. He was very self-assured. Kauto Star and Denman were best mates when they went out in a field. They enjoyed each other's company.'

Nobody that I have spoken to spends more time looking at horses in a field than Ruth Carr. She says: 'I have a group of 24 and I could stand there for hours and watch them or wander round the field. When you go there some can't leave you alone and come pushing at you all the time from the other side of the fence while others don't even look up from eating grass. They are all different just like people.'

Willie Carson does the same at his stud. He also spots a pecking order. 'Mine will stay together until three weeks before the sale and then they go out one by one. They have been together since they were born and know one another. You've got the guy who says "I'm not playing with you". The others will have their little fights.'

Unlike Carr, though, he prefers to introduce a dominant gelding to act as boss. 'I always have a gelding who is in charge. I never have the yearlings on their own because if you do they will start fighting each other, but if you have an old gelding with them they are fighting for fun, not fighting to be in charge, because he is already there with them and they know it. The yearling will do "mousing", smacking his lips together.

'I put as many as I have all together. I don't mix barren mares with geldings because that would be asking for trouble but all the young stock are together. They are herd animals. They don't want to be split up into sixes like they do at Newmarket and then you get all the fighting. They gallop like crazy. My horses walk into the paddock. I have taught them from a very young age to go out quietly into the paddock and they turn round and we put head collars on and stand with them and talk to them and they mooch off in their own time. Around them you have to be fearless. You have to be the boss. You have to walk up to them and be bold. You can give them a pat on the neck and then look them in the eye and say "I'm the guvnor". I have had to learn all this.

'I have sat in my car for hours and watched horses, how they behave and what they do in the paddock. You pick up tiny bits of information and like a puzzle you put it all together. I am still learning.'

Carson learnt how important it was to take charge during his years in the saddle. He says: 'When I rode a horse and was given a leg up in the paddock I picked up the reins – I didn't know I was doing it early on – but I sort of squeezed the horse and got a tight hold of the rein and looked him in the eye and gave a whistle – "I'm in charge boy no worries" – and I was very confident. The horse then relaxed. If that horse knows you are in charge he will relax. He says "you're in charge, so I'm all right". I was the tiniest jockey in the weighing room but found I could hold the strongest pullers going to post.'

Declan Murphy also talks of taking charge. 'It is because most horses are subservient that when you sit on them as a rider you know that you can get that horse to trust in you. There is a bond that develops in that moment and the horse will do anything for you. He trusts in you because he believes in you.'

There is an element of mind games about the bonding process. Ronnie Postlethwaite says: 'I think you must let a horse think that it's all his idea. If he thinks he is enjoying it, great, let him carry on doing it.'

Gary Witheford stresses the importance of the horse recognising you as the leader, and he has a technique that helps them accept that. 'None of my horses ever walk at my side,' he says. 'They walk behind me. We take that protection away from a foal if we make it walk beside us. For example if you want to load a horse onto a trailer, if its head is ahead of you it will think "you are not going up there so why should I?" The brushes come out and people start to swear, but actually the horse is protecting itself because the leader is not going there. Once it sees you as a leader it will start to do things within seconds.

'If a horse doesn't fit in the herd and is rejected because it is weak, sick or elderly that is when the lions, tigers and wolves take it out. The way I work is that horses are looking for a leader. When that happens it starts to do things differently. Horses are sent to me because the leadership has gone. My job is to become their leader.'

The dominant horse of the herd can find itself threatened on occasions, but not always in the manner you would expect. Sir Mark Prescott says: 'In the herd, as with all herds, they put up with being bossed around by one until they think they get half a chance of beating him up. So if the stallion goes lame or loses his powers he is quickly shoved out. The stallion in the herd is in the middle. He is not galloping down the valley in the lead like you see in westerns or the Lloyds Bank advertisements. The dominant male is in the middle and he makes sure that he stays in the middle. The predators kill the ones on the outside. They are the ones that sink into the quicksand. As he grows old he in turn is shoved to the outside and gets killed so the natural place for the horse to be, if he can, is in the middle of the herd.'

Witheford, however, says the dominant horse of the herd is not always the main target of the challengers for the top. He says: 'It's not the alpha that gets beaten up. It's the number two that wants to be alpha that gets beaten up as it is normally protecting the alpha male in the herd. It's the one which is fighting to get to the top. People come and tell me that their horse is the alpha and always getting into fights but it is generally not the case, it is the second, who is protecting the number one. It doesn't want to have to look round for another leader.'

Rather like people in a crowded room it is not necessarily the loud and brash person that holds sway. Some champion racehorses have been quiet and very reserved types. By contrast the alpha in the herd may simply be a bully or the strongest physically.

Racing is, through the competitive nature of the sport, a meritocracy. The best are encouraged to beat the best. Yet unlike in the wild, where the weakest is most at risk, in the environment of the stable the gifted handler has the chance to restore the balance and encourage the less able or less gifted to flourish. That is, ultimately, the horseman's primary duty of care.

9

Just the Stubs

A good trainer can hear a horse speak to him. A great trainer can hear it whisper. Monty Roberts

One of the most memorable encounters that I have ever seen on the racetrack took place in the 1975 King George VI and Queen Elizabeth Diamond Stakes between Grundy and Bustino.

In what is still described by many as the greatest race they ever saw, there was an unhappy postscript. Neither of the main protagonists reproduced that level of ability again. In fact one of them sustained an injury from which he never recovered.

The 4/5 favourite for the race was Grundy, a colt that his trainer Peter Walwyn described as 'blond, beautiful and the most marvellous mover' when he first saw him as a yearling at the Overbury Stud. Walwyn trained Grundy to finish second in the 2,000 Guineas and go one better in the Irish equivalent before winning the Derby at Epsom by three lengths, a race run in front of a crowd reported to have numbered quarter of a million people. Three weeks later the dashing chestnut won the Irish Derby at the Curragh by two lengths.

His main rival for the King George was Bustino, a four-year-old that had won the previous year's St Leger. Yet this was no two-horse race, as they were joined by Eclipse Stakes winner Star Appeal, who would subsequently win the Prix de l'Arc de Triomphe, the previous

Ascot 1975 – Grundy defeats the gallant Bustino

year's Irish Oaks winner Dibidale and the charismatic French mare Dahlia, who had won the King George in 1973 and 1974.

Major Dick Hern, trainer of Bustino, took the unusual step of employing two stablemates – Highest and Kinglet – to act as pacemakers and ensure a strong gallop for his confirmed stayer. The race went according to plan in the early stages, as Highest led Kinglet by two lengths with Bustino tracking them in third. Kinglet then took over as Star Appeal moved into second before Bustino took up the running half a mile from home. Pat Eddery and Grundy tracked him in second and looked held as they passed the two-furlong marker but, with Eddery riding at his strongest, he moved alongside a furlong out and managed to edge ahead to win by half a length, with Dahlia five lengths back in third.

What looked a scorching pace to the eye was confirmed by the clock, with the winning time of 2min 26.98 breaking the track record by almost two and a half seconds – a record that was to stand until Harbinger won the same race, round a slightly modified track, in 2010 in a time of 2min 26.78. One scribe wrote afterwards that it was a race that brought 'grown men to tears'.

Afterwards both horses appeared close to collapse. Joe Mercer, rider of Bustino, reported that his horse broke down in the closing stages. He was never to race again. 'Until Grundy got to us well inside the distance, I think he had the race won, but then he changed his legs, lost a bit of momentum and Grundy wore him down,' he reported.

Peter Walwyn said he felt 'numb' after watching what he still describes as the best race he ever saw. Afterwards Dick Hern came to congratulate him and when the press asked Walwyn about future plans, he replied 'to the bar for a large one'. Brough Scott has never forgotten what he says was 'the hardest, most implacable, most moving Flat race I have ever seen'.

Major Dick Hern – trainer of Bustino

Peter Walwyn – masterful handler of Grundy

Grundy returned home very tired but was 'bouncing again within three days', according to his trainer, so he ran once more in what was then known as the Benson and Hedges Gold Cup at York, but he trailed home fourth behind Dahlia, Card King and Star Appeal – all of whom he had beaten comfortably at Ascot. He was retired to stud, siring Oaks winner Bireme, before being exported to Japan where he died in 1992.

Walwyn says: 'Grundy appeared to have come out of the race very well, but then Shergar appeared to be all right before the St Leger and Troy appeared to be all right before the Arc. When horses go over the top it can be very hard to judge it. The last person who knows is the trainer because you're watching them every day and think they are all right. When you give a horse a Classic preparation you need to be doing swinging canters by the middle of March, and it's very hard to keep them going throughout the season.'

I remember the first ever time I felt saddened by the outcome of a race.

It was 1970 and I had taken a keen interest in the career of Nijinsky, who had become the first horse for 35 years to complete the English Triple Crown – the 2,000 Guineas, the Derby and the St Leger. His next race was the Prix de l'Arc de Triomphe, run at Longchamp in October, and to my great dismay he was beaten a head by Sassafras, ridden by the great French champion Yves Saint-Martin. Nijinsky's rider Lester Piggott reported afterwards that the colt was past his peak, so it was surprising to see him asked to race again a fortnight later in the Champion Stakes. Sweating and nervous beforehand, he was again beaten and was then retired to stud in Kentucky.

There have been dozens of occasions when a horse has been asked to run one race too many. Troy, winner of eight races including the Derby, Irish Derby, King George VI and Queen Elizabeth Diamond Stakes and the Benson and Hedges Gold Cup, started odds-on to win the Prix de l'Arc de Triomphe but struggled to finish third. Shergar flopped in the St Leger, possibly failing to stay the 1m 6f trip although many took the view, including Lester Piggott, that the colt was probably 'over the top' by that time of the season.

Sir Mark Prescott believes that every horse has a limited amount it can give. He uses the analogy of a cheque book, with each horse holding a finite number of cheques.

'You don't know how much the horse has got in the account when you start but every time you run the horse you are, metaphorically speaking, writing a cheque. Then it suddenly bounces. Sometimes you begin to get a few warning signals – for example the horse may start to get sweaty at home – and you begin to see the way the wind is blowing. The horse may hang on for a couple more races. In all sports based on courage all participants one day say no. It is the cumulative effect of that drawing on reserves of courage. Matadors, boxers, jockeys, dogs and horses all cry "enough" eventually.'

The size of 'the account' varies enormously from horse to horse. Some horses simply can't hack it at all and never see the track. Others can have remarkably long careers. During my lifetime I can recall a grand old chaser named Sonny Somers, twice winning over fences in 1980 at the age of 18. John Francome rode him on occasions – barely older than the horse himself. In modern times Victory Gunner raced at the age of 17, having won 14 of his 83 lifetime races. Fiddlers Pike was 16 when he ran at Newton Abbot in 1997 but the horse I recall most vividly was a grand old warrior named Mac Vidi. In 1980, aged 15, he became the oldest horse to be placed in the Cheltenham Gold Cup, finishing third to Master Smudge and Tied Cottage before being promoted to second. He was bred out of a mare that cost just £100 and was a late bloomer, winning eight of his last 11 starts in handicaps before that thrilling effort in the Gold Cup.

One horse that did not appear to 'say no' was Sea The Stars, who in 2009 won eight of his nine starts including a Group 1 over trips ranging from a mile to a mile and a half every month, from May to October, of his three-year-old career. His trainer John Oxx knew from an early stage that the colt had a more substantial pool of resources than most horses. He says:

'Sea The Stars had that physical and mental constitution. Not many have. We knew from the word go that this fellow could keep going from race to race and undergo a busy campaign because he had great physical strength, energy and a tremendous appetite. He just slept and ate. He was also very sound. He was beautifully put together – a big well-grown horse. He ate everything that was put in front of him and would come out a ball of energy the next day. He would always need a lot of walking before he left the yard. We gave him plenty of exercise to burn that energy off.

'He was cantering within a couple of days of a race and soon went back into fast work. We intentionally missed the King George with him because we wanted to go for the Guineas, Derby and Eclipse and then the Juddmonte, Irish Champion Stakes and the Arc. He never had a holiday, though. He just cantered instead of doing fast work and went out every day, always fresh and well. After he won the Arc he looked better than ever at home and the lad riding him said, "Boss, he needs another race. He's ready to go again!" Now that is very unusual.'

Sea The Stars was exceptional, because he managed to maintain his level of form in the highest grade through a season.

Denman, who was nicknamed 'The Tank' due to his imposing physique, may have been another. Dan Skelton worked as assistant trainer to Paul Nicholls when Kauto Star and Denman were in the yard.

'Denman ran his heart out in the 2008 Gold Cup, exhausting himself to such a level that he became exceptionally tired, but then he defied all the rules because he came back to win a Hennessy under 11st 12lb and finish second in three more Gold Cups. Denman and

Denman – 'The Tank' in full flight

Cityscape – winning the 2012 Dubai Duty Free

Kauto Star were so good that they didn't really take as much out of their "bank account" as horses of lesser ability. Most horses have a hard day at the races but because they were superior to the opposition they got over their races better. There were only a few opportunities for them to run so they could be looked after between races.

'It's almost as if the better you are, the better the life you have. A horse of that quality may only have to exert itself at a very high level three times a year whereas the lesser horse will get a harder time in races he will struggle to win. The limitations are there.'

In more recent times Cityscape is an example of a horse that pushed himself to the limit on one big occasion. That was in the 2012 Dubai Duty Free, run at Meydan in March and worth almost £2 million to the winner. Cityscape tracked the leaders before kicking clear quarter of a mile from home and drawing away to win by just over four lengths, beating the previous course record by 0.09sec.

Cityscape ran six more times and although he finished second twice and third, another victory eluded him.

His trainer Roger Charlton says: 'Nobody expected him to break the course record or be so sensational. It's probably fair to say he didn't ever do it again, but on the night it was a super effort. It can be a pretty gut-wrenching experience and sometimes they simply don't recover.'

Had the horse given any indication at home that he may have had enough? 'He was an interesting case,' says Charlton, 'We trained him here at Beckhampton and he went out to Dubai seven days before the race. The weather here was fine so we could do the work we needed. We thought it would be easier for him here. Had we been training him on a fast surface in Dubai he might not have been prepared to let himself go on the night. He had never been put under pressure on that track before. Some horses may come back and cope with fast ground but if you keep asking them to work on an unforgiving surface they may turn round and say "I've given it to you, I've given it to you …"'

Michael Dickinson recalls one notable example of a horse that didn't come back.

'Dorlesa won 16 races for me as a jockey including the Benson and Hedges Chase at Sandown and not once, in the seven seasons he raced, did I hit him behind the saddle because he gave his all every time. At Chepstow one day he was carrying over 12 stone and was conceding over a stone to several good horses. Before the race we didn't think that he could win and at the third last I asked him to come with a run. He gave everything and took the lead but then going to the last jump I felt him cut out. He made it to the line and just held on but he never won another race. He was diagnosed with a strained heart after the race having thrown his whole body on the line for me. That was the last race he ever won.'

Ruth Carr seldom asks much of her horses at home. 'We would do a lot less on the gallops than most trainers which is why our horses can get more miles on the clock. That is why our old horses keep on going for us.'

Jim Bolger's horses have a reputation for toughness. However in the case of Alexander Goldrun, who won him five Group 1 races, there may have been a reason why she kept going so long. She was a leading player in the 2006 Nassau Stakes – a race that has been compared by some with the Grundy/Bustino clash.

'She is an interesting example because she never gave it all,' says Bolger. 'She probably gave 98 per cent. She always managed to keep a bit back for herself, notably in that Nassau Stakes when she was short-headed by Ouija Board. I was thrilled with the ride Kevin Manning gave her and I am sure that Ed Dunlop was just as thrilled with the ride that Frankie Dettori gave the winner. This was, for me, the fillies' equivalent of the Grundy/ Bustino encounter. My filly didn't win again but she ran some good races, probably because she never really made the supreme effort in her life.'

There are many possible reasons why a horse might struggle to come back to top form after a very hard race. Bolger says: 'It could well be that the horses involved have little problems, here and there, and the pain gets worse when they make that extra effort and then they simply decide they are not going to do it again. They just don't have the reserves to do it. Perhaps with six months' rest they could come back but the good Flat horses may be going off to stud because the connections may have commercial considerations at the front of their minds. I don't think there is an owner in the world who doesn't keep an eye on the bottom line as to what his champion is worth. Sometimes it is not the horse that doesn't come back. It's the trainer or owner that doesn't come back.'

That was certainly the case with Robert Sangster in the 1970s, where commercial considerations were always uppermost in his mind. Try My Best, for example, was the champion two-year-old of 1977 and following an early trial on his three-year-old debut, which he won, he was syndicated for US $6 million. The colt then finished last in the 2,000 Guineas and never raced again. He did, though, do well at stud siring Group winners Last Tycoon, Waajib and My Best Valentine.

The 1989 2,000 Guineas and Derby winner Nashwan struggled to recapture his best form after beating Opening Verse in the Eclipse Stakes at Sandown. He had to work really hard to win that race and although he went on to beat Cacoethes by a neck a fortnight later, he only ran once more.

John Gosden believes a demanding career on the track can affect a horse beyond its racing days.

'Federico Tesio, breeder of the great Ribot, alluded to a finite supply of nervous energy. He said that fillies should not be over-raced because they would not produce. Indeed a lot of people say that the great race fillies show many masculine traits and might not be able to give to a foal as readily when they become a broodmare as, say, the unraced full sister. So there is an argument that if you over-race them they won't be able to produce.

'It is the same with great jump jockeys. You only have to stand at the last open ditch to see the speed they jump and hear the noise. Those riders have to be beyond fearless. They have to be a different type of human being. But there will come a stage, to use the cheque book analogy, that they have written so many cheques that one day they find the book is empty. Just the stubs. They have had to show a level of mental and physical courage that few of us can aspire to. I would not suggest that they lose it – more that it is literally exhausted. There comes a stage when you walk into the room, put the tack down and walk away.'

Federico Tesio – one of racing's most profound thinkers

Peter Makin thinks of another example from the sporting world. "When we won the Rugby World Cup in Australia you will remember Jonny Wilkinson made that kick in the last couple of minutes but something in him seemed to die after that. He couldn't really do anything like that again. I had a horse called Pivotal Point who had a tremendous season in 2004, winning four times including a Group 3 and Group 2. I then ran him in Hong Kong and he only won one more race. He was totally burnt out. I think the journey and the race took too much out of him.'

Henry Candy differentiates between the mental and physical side. He says: 'I am not sure how much of it is mental and how much is just "petrol in the tank". There is a finite amount that any horse can give.

But take any sportsman. Usain Bolt is not going to run 50 times a year. He and his trainers know he can only produce an amazing performance a limited number of times over a limited number of years. That is more physical than mental although the two are closely connected. Whether the bank account is in the head or just the physical effort I don't know. I suspect it is 25 per cent brain and 75 per cent body. It is too simplistic to say that as you get older you can do less having used up an awful lot of energy, but there is an element of that with horses.'

Peter Scudamore questions whether a human athlete should be compared with the equine. He says: 'When I rode for Martin Pipe he used to say that you must not compare a human athlete with an equine one. The experience of a hard race can be a mental thing as well as physical. I can think of National Hunt horses that were better novices than they were later in their careers because they had hard races and didn't want to do it again. Part of the jockey's skill is to persuade them to overcome that.'

William Haggas produced one of the best training performances of recent years when he sent out Shaamit to win the 1996 Derby on his seasonal debut. The colt then ran three more times, putting up a good effort to finish third in the King George VI and Queen Elizabeth Diamond Stakes, but he failed to win another race.

'Shaamit never really reproduced his Derby form afterwards. I would attribute that to my inexperience as a trainer but he gave it all that day. He ran well at Ascot but was a bit flat in the Irish Champion Stakes and he then got a leg in the Arc. But running first time out in the Derby, on that track, is what did for him.'

The King George in which Shaamit finished third was won by Pentire, a race that his rider Michael Hills believes got to the bottom of him.

'That was a remarkable race by Pentire. He was left about eight lengths at the start but he moved up to challenge a quarter of a mile from home and stayed on well to beat Classic Cliche by one and three-quarter lengths, with Shaamit a further neck back in third.'

Hills, as with the others jockeys I've talked to, makes the point that at the end of a long season the horse may be carrying an injury of some kind.

'I would agree that a horse may have a limited amount to give,' he says, 'but then I would also mention injuries. When a horse puts in a massive effort it may pull a muscle or damage a tendon, and that may be the reason why they don't do it again. It would not be because it bust their heart. If a young horse injures itself – a pelvis would be a good example – I promise you it can take 20 per cent out of them. So they may have six months off but they are never as good as they could have been.'

Peter Scudamore rode many great racehorses in his time and many of them had problems of one type or another.

'Granville Again won the Champion Hurdle in 1993 and never won another race because he broke blood vessels. If you went on him too soon he would break blood vessels. He was extremely talented and the trick was to challenge when the other horses were tiring. If you challenged too early and he came under pressure he wouldn't face it. Pearlyman was probably the most talented horse I ever rode. He won the Queen Mother Champion Chase in successive years. He had supreme class and speed. I suspect sometimes he felt his legs which is why he didn't always jump that well. If you let Pearlyman's head go he would put down on you. You had to keep contact with him and then he would come up.'

Declan Murphy believes that Deep Sensation was never the same horse after getting a very hard race to win the Tote Gold Trophy, even though he went on to win the Queen Mother Champion Chase.

'He won the Queen Mother with two stone up his sleeve! That horse had so much ability. The key was that you could never allow him to believe he was in a race. Because of that hard race at Newbury

Deep Sensation – on his way to victory at Cheltenham

he had no trust in his own potential or ability. He was reluctant to give anything because he had passed the pain threshold.'

There are few races more gruelling than the Grand National, even though recent modifications to the fences have put less emphasis on jumping prowess than was formerly the case. One trend relating to this subject is the subsequent record of recent Grand National winners. You have to go back to 2002 for the last horse to win the Grand National and then win another race under rules. That was Bindaree, who the following season won the Welsh Grand National, but since then up to the spring of 2014 not one of the subsequent 12 winners has won another race under rules.

Dr Richard Newland, trainer of 2014 Grand National winner Pineau De Re, says: 'In the case of the Grand National the poor record can often be related to the horse's subsequent higher mark in the handicap. Pineau De Re is now rated on 151, which is high for an 11-year-old going on 12. Pineau De Re has gained his mark on the basis of running four and a half miles over 30 fences but there is no

Pineau De Re – clear winner of the 2014 Grand National

other race of this type he can run in. The race attracts 40 horses all in the handicap so for a horse to come back and run second or third is pretty remarkable off a higher weight. I am a big fan of Red Rum, but when he came back to win it twice more there were usually only a dozen or so horses in the handicap and you could virtually put a line through 20 of them. Now the race is worth £1 million and there are 40 good horses all in the weights.'

Newland does, though, agree that it's possible to ask too much of a horse. 'I definitely think that if you take horses to the well and they give their all for you then for a lot of them it is a painful experience.'

Yet, like Hills, he argues that there can be a physical reason for a horse's loss of form. He says, 'Someone did a study that showed after scoping all the horses in a race, 60 per cent of them bled. Now bleeding is not much fun for a horse. If they bleed torrentially their lungs will fill and they struggle to breathe. It is not unlike the sensation of drowning. Sometimes those are the horses that become known as 'thinkers'. They will plop around in fourth gear but won't move into fifth because they have learnt that when they do so they may face that bad experience again. They are as happy as Larry in their comfort zone but ask them for more and they will sit there and not give it to you.'

Paul Nicholls believes a lot comes down to the constitution of the individual horse.

'I can tell you that Call Equiname didn't come back after winning the Champion Chase in 1999. He ran four more times, finishing third twice, but he wasn't the same horse. You do get horses that reach a peak but the race breaks their spirit and they may never do it again. It's all about knowing them as individuals. I always say that it can take two years to get to know a horse properly. You never stop learning about them and just have to do what you instinctively feel is right.

'See More Business won us 18 races including the 1999 Gold Cup and he was still winning races when he was 13. He even ran in the Gold Cup that year. Kauto Star won five King Georges and two Gold Cups and he was still running when he was 12. Neptune Collonges won the Grand National aged 11 and Tidal Bay was still running creditably aged 13.'

Oliver Sherwood spent his early days working with the great Fred Winter. He can recall an occasion when a horse never recovered from a gruelling race.

'I have known occasions when the runner-up in a race has had its heart broken. My brother Simon rode Desert Orchid for a while and we had a horse at Fred's called Ihaventalight. Fred thought the world of this horse and everyone in the yard backed it but it got beaten first time by Desert Orchid. Unlike Fred he decided to take the winner, who had a penalty, on again and he told John Francome that the weight difference would tell but he was beaten again. Ihaventalight eventually won a fair race but he needed blinkers and we were always adamant that Desert Orchid broke his heart.'

Trainers have to be at their most perceptive, especially towards the end of a season, for any signs that their horse has had enough. One strange phenomenon that can happen in the autumn is for a horse to do a brilliant piece of work prior to running poorly.

Henry Candy has seen it more than once. He says: 'I have made that mistake so many times, especially towards the end of the year when the horse is slightly over the top. Perfectly ordinary horses will suddenly produce a fantastic piece of work and so I run it again and it runs atrociously. I think the horse is probably working on its nerves. At the end of the year when they know they can't cope with another race then they will do too much and run away from something at home and you can mistake that for a brilliant piece of work.'

Roger Charlton has seen the same. 'Yes that does happen. A piece of work can be the most misleading thing. You can have a 90-rated horse working with a 60-rated horse and the 60-rated works really well but then runs to 60. I find that you need to eliminate the variable. The more horses you work in a group the more reliable the form book is because it is more like a race.'

John Gosden says: 'The so-called "over the top" thing is more a European Northern Hemisphere issue. When you have taken a horse and trained it from early February in bad weather, have picked it up and run it in a Classic early in the year – and you must remember that we have run four of the Classics by the official end of spring – then suddenly you have the mid-season programme and the three-year-old is asked to take on the older horses. Not surprisingly if they haven't had a holiday they are bound to get pretty drained.

'Horses are not fully mature until they are four and a Flat racer, if it is sound and healthy, may not be at its peak until it is five. When you get to the autumn of the year in Europe remember the days are shortening and the light is shorter and horses change their coats. It is not the changing of the coat which is the issue though. It's the sign of hormonal fluctuations in that horse as well as the climatic change.

'Why do you put a mare under lights to get her to ovulate? You are teasing her into thinking that it is spring and early summer when it is not. So hormonally they will change with the seasons and race according to that. Strange to relate that some fillies will race into the autumn because the hormonal nightmare for them has been the spring and by the autumn all that has settled down. It was always different when I was in California. You could race a horse for 18 months straight because the seasons were so subtle there and the weather always pleasant. That is very different. I always say that here we train a lot around climate and in some parts of the world they don't have to contend with that. That is a big factor.'

Luca Cumani says: 'It could be that the superb gallop was too hard and close to the race which is why the horse didn't run well. That could happen any time through the season. Then if the horse runs badly it is easy to say that it was over the top. Horses can easily lose their race on the gallops and not have sufficient time to recover.'

Michael Hills rode thousands of horses in work during his career. He believes that a sparkling gallop at the end of the season can be due to a kind of 'last gasp'. He says: 'It can happen when they have had a long campaign and they start to worry about their work because it's getting harder. They are feeling their work more and they give a big effort and that's when they go. The good ones have their work easy all year and suddenly they are finding it harder because they need a rest. And they start to fret and then do a massive piece of work. It's a sign they are coming to an end. You have to pick up on it.'

The training of a racehorse requires deep insight into the horse's mental and physical condition, no more so than at the end of a tough campaign. Appearances, though, can clearly be deceptive. As Tesio suggested every horse has a finite amount of resources, and the trainer's job is to spot how much it has at an early stage and then plan its career accordingly.

10

The Inner Sanctum

A true horseman does not look at the horse with his eyes,
he looks at the horse with his heart. Unknown

If you're going to make a fool of yourself then you may as well do it in style and, from a racing perspective, there is no better place to do so than at Epsom on Derby Day.

Back in 1989 I was writing a column entitled 'Warm Up' for *The Sunday Times*. My brief was to look ahead to the week's racing, offering advice to the readers with special reference to the big races. The feature was proving popular and I was not afraid to take a view, occasionally advising horses at very long prices. Some of them had won, so my confidence was sky high.

I also liked to swim against the tide when it came to short-priced favourites and, for a reason that I can no longer recall, in the spring of 1989 I decided that Nashwan's one-length defeat of Exbourne in the 2,000 Guineas did not warrant his short price for the Derby. Looking back I can't think what came over me, as the colt had the pedigree to stay the trip and the class to win. Furthermore, he was trained by Major Dick Hern and ridden by Willie Carson, both of whom knew a good horse when they saw one.

It soon became apparent that I stood virtually isolated in my view, with colleagues from the press room in the weeks leading up to the big race taking every opportunity to advise me that my judgement was seriously awry. It seemed that each and every one of them had backed Nashwan to win the Derby and, to make things worse, they had done so when the odds were considerably more attractive. Indeed, a few of them had taken 33/1 about the colt winning both the 2,000 Guineas and the Derby.

What made things worse was that I had every opportunity to rectify the situation because I occasionally did corporate work alongside Willie Carson, speaking to business clients in private boxes before the start of the day's racing.

We must have looked a strange partnership – I stand at 6ft 4ins and Willie does not – but between us we did a good job for the punters and, on Derby Day 1989, we found ourselves sharing a helicopter from Ascot to Epsom Downs. As it was a long walk from the landing strip to the grandstand I offered to carry Willie's bag, with his whip, so he could concentrate on talking to the members of the public who were stopping him for a quick chat.

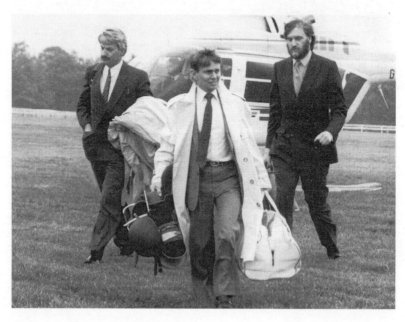

Derby Day 1989 – a great double act

The Derby had concentrated my mind for the weeks leading up to the race. I woke up thinking about Nashwan and I went to sleep thinking about him. Come the day I had never wished so hard for a horse to lose. But that was never going to happen. As soon as Carson kicked for home two furlongs out the race was over, as he pulled five lengths clear of the 500/1 outsider Terimon.

As I walked towards the weighing room after the race to find Willie someone brushed past me hissing the word 'Nashwan' – I turned around quickly but he was lost in the crowd. To this day I have no idea who it was. Willie and I made our way back over the Downs for the helicopter trip home. I feigned delight at his success, but not very well.

The ultimate ignominy had been to carry his wretched bag. In that act of kindness I had been party to my humiliating fall from grace. It took me weeks to recover.

Nashwan – striding home in the 1989 Derby

The Nashwan story had begun a couple of months earlier at West Ilsley. Successful in both his starts as a two-year-old, the following spring he was not actually rated the yard's leading hope for the year's Classics. A colt named Prince Of Dance, who had dead-heated in the previous autumn's Dewhurst Stakes, was considered their number one candidate for top honours.

Carson told me how it was that Nashwan first came to the forefront of the scene. 'There were three horses in the gallop and I was on Nashwan. I went back to our top work-rider Brian Proctor, who was on another horse, and asked him at the end of the gallop why he had pulled up and they all looked puzzled and he said "we didn't pull up". I said "I beat you a furlong" and the horse I beat was a highly-rated four-year-old. We knew Nashwan was a good horse – that was never in doubt – but that was the first time we realised he was a superstar. That told us we had something special.'

'One of our owners, Arnold Weinstock, had come to see his horse Prince Of Dance work, possibly the best horse I ever rode. He was going to be our Guineas horse and this was supposed to be his last piece of work before the race, but the horse went lame and couldn't work and so we upgraded Nashwan, who worked in his place. That's why Arnold was there. Anyway he had one of those new-fangled mobile telephones that in those days was the size of a brick and I said you're the lucky man because you can get on the telephone to have a bet and I think he did.'

Nashwan has a special place in Carson's heart, but there were others. 'Bireme, who won the 1980 Oaks, was one of the best fillies I ever rode. Little Wolf was like a bulldozer – he just kept going – and Troy was impressive when he won the Derby but was quite a dull sort of horse.'

Another occasion when the potential for a life-changing bet presented itself was when a colt named Shaamit was pitched into a piece of work with leading fancies for the 1996 Derby. Shaamit had not been entered for the race originally and it was only after Lester Piggott, father-in-law of trainer William Haggas, rode the colt in an exercise gallop that he was added to the race as a supplementary entry. He would have run before Epsom in the Dante Stakes at York but was withdrawn after sustaining a setback.

Michael Hills, who rode the colt at Epsom, takes up the story: 'His work was unbelievable before the race. He was such an honest horse. Some horses that you ride keep giving and giving. He probably gave too much that day in the Derby. The day after he couldn't even walk out of his box he was so stiff. His soundness was great but he had got ringworm before the Dante which doesn't sound much but it can affect a horse big time. That is why he missed the Dante so William trained him straight for the Derby. We worked him with Henry Cecil's Dushyantor, who was then favourite for the race, and also with the Dante winner from Paul Kelleway's yard named Glory Of Dancer, and he beat them. He only had to reproduce his homework and we knew he had a shout.'

There is something rather special about feeling you get close to the 'inner sanctum'. Because I could not afford to keep a horse in training myself I formed syndicates with trainers that interested me – specifically for that reason. There were certain names that were mentioned in reverential tones – well-respected work-riders or lads – and one name that stopped you in your tracks was Alan Bailey.

Bailey was the leading work-rider for Peter Walwyn, who was twice champion trainer in 1974 and 1975. Walwyn had sent out Humble Duty to win the 1,000 Guineas, Polygamy to win the Oaks and the mighty Grundy to win the 1975 Epsom Derby. Walwyn was 'the man', and Bailey would know what he'd had for breakfast.

Yet, despite being linked to those great names, the best horse Bailey ever rode on the home gallops hardly created a ripple – let alone a splash – in the history of the game. His name was Lunchtime.

Lunchtime – a horse of great talent

'The best horse I ever sat on in my life was Lunchtime,' says Bailey. 'He is the only horse that made my hair stand on end. He sent a tingle down my spine. You couldn't judge pace on him. If you sat four lengths behind in a piece of work you would go to move up and in a few strides be six lengths clear. He was a brilliant horse. He was unbeaten at two – winning the 1972 Dewhurst – but then Boldboy beat him in the Greenham and he didn't do a tap. He was colty afterwards and it turned out that he had a bad heart. He was the quickest learner I ever knew. You only needed to show him something once but I never sat on anything like him in my life.'

Bailey had loads of punters – people to put money on for him – and stories of his touches became the stuff of legend. His main man was John Banks, a fearless bookmaker who dominated the betting ring. Bailey says: 'That is how I got to know John Banks. I was in the Rutland Hotel at Newmarket having a drink and he asked if I was

Alan Bailey. He asked me if Lunchtime would win the Guineas and I said "no", and he said "thank God otherwise I would be signing cheques until this time next year."'

Lunchtime did not realise his full potential on the track due to a physical issue. One horse that did was Spindrifter. Many years ago the racing programme offered more opportunity for horses on the Flat to build up a sequence of victories. Few trainers can match Sir Mark Prescott's knowledge of the racing calendar and Spindrifter, who was to win 10 races in succession during the 1980 season, could not have been in better hands.

The son of Sandford Lad was bred by Joe Crowley, father of Aidan O'Brien's wife Anne-Marie. During the summer of 1980 he won 13 races and only once finished out of the first two in 19 starts. His victories mainly came at northern and Scottish tracks. He met his end the following season as a result of a freak accident on the gallops, when he was kicked above the knee by another horse and fractured his off-fore.

Typically Prescott had a plan for the horse from an early stage in the horse's life. He says: 'I was very lucky to have Spindrifter and lucky to have Mr Waters as an owner. I asked him if he wanted to win a lot of races or have a crack at the Windsor Castle at Royal Ascot because what you can't do is change your mind halfway. What do you want to do? He opted for a lot of races.

'I felt that Spindrifter was some way below the top, and I was right as he only got 7st 13lb in the Free Handicap at the end of the season, having won 13 races. Only 7st 13lb! So that gives you an idea of how much placing helped him, but after his third run I was aware that he was unbelievably tough, very sound and loved hard ground, which was much more prevalent in those days, and the programme book had left me the opportunity to exploit those qualities.'

Further Flight – as tough as they get

Another multiple winner, a few years later, was Further Flight. Barry Hills trained the grey, who was ridden by his son Michael, who told me: 'I got very attached to Further Flight because we were together a long time and I remember getting quite emotional when I realised that I was never going to ride him again. The way dad kept Further Flight's enthusiasm for nine years was amazing. I won 22 races on him from riding him 64 times. Great horse, great trainer, great jockey!'

What can be perceived as well-laid plans can sometimes simply be a consequence of circumstances. Luca Cumani enjoys a reputation for being a very shrewd placer of a horse, and I was intrigued to know the story of Presvis, who started his winning career from a handicap mark of 72 and ended up winning over £4 million in prize-money including the Group 1 QE II Cup at Sha Tin and the Dubai Duty Free Cup at Meydan. Cumani put his judgement on the line with Presvis, having persuaded the owner to wait until the horse was four before allowing him to see the racetrack.

'Presvis started in handicaps because he was a terribly unsound horse at two and three and didn't race until he was four. When I started with him I was not confident of giving him much work and therefore he started when he was only 70 per cent fit. I had tested the owner's patience in keeping him unraced until he was four and was trying everything possible for him not to go wrong again before he got to the racecourse. When he returned from a race sound and stayed sound I became bolder and started training him more to try and make him fitter and better.'

Cumani has trained the winners of many of the world's top races, including two Derbys, an Arlington Million and a Japan Cup, and one of his best horses was Falbrav, who won at the highest level in the UK, France and Hong Kong. He says: 'Falbrav was already a made horse when he joined me. He improved further and horses can improve up to the age of five if they haven't been exploited and that is what he did. He looked pretty ordinary when he came and started cantering and it wasn't until I asked him for something serious that he looked special. That is why I always say I don't judge a horse until I have seen it galloping. People ask me how a two-year-old is before it has galloped and I always say it looks fine at the moment, but if you and I went jogging with Linford Christie we would look fine but if we went on the blocks we wouldn't.'

A few years later, on the other side of the pond, Michael Dickinson was showing that he had lost none of his touch with his masterful handling of Da Hoss, who won the Breeders' Cup Mile in 1996 and then again two years later in 1998, despite having just one race in between.

He says: 'We never lost faith in Da Hoss despite the myriad problems he encountered,' he told me. 'Da Hoss was our life – our reason for being. That was not only me but our head man Miguel Piedra, his exercise rider Jon-Boy Ferriday, and Joan Wakefield.

Da Hoss – 'easy' was never an option

Miguel would spend at least three hours every day with him. Da Hoss was full of character and he loved to train. In fact he loved to train almost too much. If he had been a person I would have told him if you don't feel right take it easy, but easy was never on Da Hoss's itinerary. He was a strong character, bossy and playful. A horse with his ability and character you don't give up. We knew if we could get him to the races he would do the rest.

'When a top vet informed us that he wouldn't make the first small race, let alone the Breeders' Cup, he was probably correct. Miguel Piedra came to me after that report and said "Don't worry, we will get him there". We always had belief. It did help that we had a marvellous Tapeta gallop and three brilliant turf tracks to train on, one for drought weather, one for normal weather and a Noah's Ark which was good going after 11 inches of rain. Da Hoss was turned out every day in a nice two-acre grass field with lots of grass and his best friend was a 10-year-old gelding named Boomer.'

Jim Bolger had great affection for a mare named Noora Abu, who was born in 1982. She made extraordinary improvement from her first race to winning the Pretty Polly Stakes as a seven-year-old in 1989.

'Noora Abu started off in what were then called "upside-down handicaps" and on her third-last run at the Curragh she won the Group 2 Pretty Polly Stakes. That would be the equivalent these days of going from a rating of 50 to 125, which is massive improvement, but she always kept a little bit for herself as well. That is the sort of animal that will last longer. Of all the ones I have trained the one which has given me the most satisfaction is Noora Abu as she was bought very cheaply and did so well, winning 13 races.'

One of my favourite mares was Time Charter who, as a three-year-old in 1982, won the Oaks, Sun Chariot Stakes and Champion Stakes. Then the following season she won the King George VI and Queen Elizabeth Diamond Stakes and the Prix Foy before returning

Time Charter – one of my favourite mares

as a five-year-old in 1984 to win the Coronation Cup. On that last occasion she quickened impressively to beat the previous year's Oaks winner Sun Princess by five lengths. Time Charter proved a success at stud, foaling seven individual winners including a couple that won at Group level.

Candy says: 'Time Charter had boundless enthusiasm. Ninety-nine per cent of horses will tell you that they don't want to do it anymore, usually before they become five-year-olds. To have them enthusiastic still at four and five is quite extraordinary but she just loved the whole thing. She was just a very lovely high-energy character who enjoyed competition.'

Candy also excelled in his handling of a dour battler named Master Willie. Master Willie was a different type altogether although he still improved with the passing of time. He won twice as a two-year-old in 1979 and the following season ran second in the Derby before winning the prestigious Benson and Hedges Gold Cup at York. As a four-year-old he won the Jockey Club Stakes, the Coronation Cup and the Eclipse Stakes. 'I only ran him at Newbury as a two-year-old to wake him up,' Candy told me. 'He was not doing a stroke and I thought he was taking the mick. He ended up breaking the track record which was extraordinary because he had never shown anything.'

It's not always the well-known horses that endear themselves to racing's professionals. Michael Hills grew very fond of a horse named First Island, who was trained at Newmarket in the late 1990s by Geoff Wragg. He says: 'One I did fall in love with was First Island. He won the Lockinge, a top race in Hong Kong and broke the track record in the Prince of Wales's Stakes at Royal Ascot. He also won the Sussex Stakes and was the most gorgeous horse. You could put your daughter on him. He was a gentleman.

'He was very very game. When he won the Hong Kong Cup he went to win then changed his legs and I just felt something. He had gone and was given the whole winter off. He was working really well in the spring, like his usual self, and then he went and won the Lockinge but hung across the track, which wasn't typical. We were training him for Royal Ascot and I rode a piece of work on him up the watered gallop but he fractured his leg and I think that injury had been around for a while. They operated and pinned it but he didn't survive the operation. He was such a brave horse.'

Horses that race over jumps have more chance to endear themselves to the racing public, if only because they return season after season unlike their counterparts on the Flat who, if they are top class, are likely to be whisked off to stud.

It is the old campaigners that warm the heart, and in recent times one of the most popular was a horse trained by Oliver Sherwood named Eric's Charm, who raced for eight seasons from February, 2003, until his death from a stumble at the age of 13 at Newbury in March, 2011. During that time Eric's Charm won 12 races, latterly over marathon distances and often in hock-deep ground. He was not always a sound horse but relished a battle when conditions were right, notably excelling at Sandown where he won three times.

Eric's Charm was trained throughout his career by Oliver Sherwood, but like many good horses he was not always the easiest to handle. 'I had a real soft spot for him. He was not the best horse in the world by a long shot but he was incredibly brave. He is one who would have gone over a cliff for you. I bought him as an unbroken three-year-old and he was with us until the day he died. You could almost talk to him. He would have been a complete reprobate as a youngster, running away with the lad virtually every day. He was a complete lunatic but he only had to look at a gallop to get fit. He didn't have to do much work but he was a hooligan!'

Seven-time champion jockey John Francome rode many of jump racing's most famous names in his time, but the horse for whom he singles out a special mention is Sea Image. You won't see his name up alongside the greats of the game, but Francome certainly has a soft spot for him. 'He was the toughest horse I ever rode,' he says. 'He was trained by Fred Winter and you could set your clock by him. He didn't win every time but you always knew what you were going to get. He never let you down. He would run to the line. He was tough and hardy but it didn't matter what the ground was, he would keep on galloping.'

Ronnie Postlethwaite, whose wife Charlotte held the trainer's licence, had great affection for a horse named Togg.

'He was a tiny little horse, no more than 15 hands. He jumped like a cat. When I went to Ireland to see whether I should buy him I watched him canter. He moved like a big horse and I was amazed when I got into the box and saw how small he was. I said to the owner "crikey he's not very big" and I asked "does he jump?"

'"Jump? Jump?" he said, "the biggest problem is getting him to come back down!" He won for us at Haydock and did us proud.'

Rather like when meeting someone well-known for the first time, they are seldom, in my experience, quite as you expect. Apart from the initial physical impression, after a while you get to know rather more about their inner workings – what 'makes them tick' – and there can be plenty of surprises along the way.

Talking as I have to those who have worked closely with horses, they each have stories to tell. Sometimes narratives build up around the horse – tales of massive gambles being landed or an admiration based on nothing more profound than affection. Certain people are drawn to certain people, and it's evident that the same can apply in the relationship with a racehorse.

The reasons for an attraction can be hard to define. Sometimes it may be best to just listen and not allow too much light to shine in on the mystery.

11
The End Days

If you live to be a hundred, I want to live to be a hundred minus one day so I never have to live without you. Winnie the Pooh

People handle bereavement in different ways.

I saw how people dealt with it when, as a young theology student, I occasionally accompanied my father to visit a family that had just lost a loved one.

It is tempting to make some profound comment at this point about my recollections but, in reality, my chief memory is one of endless cups of tea. Whether it was my father's parish in Leeds, which was located in a mining community, or in his subsequent living in the more affluent area of Sanderstead, south-west of London, someone would reach for the kettle within moments of us walking through the door.

People have their own ways of handling grief, but generally there are four main stages – emotional, physical, cognitive and social – and these can apply to bereavement following the loss of both a human and an animal.

The emotional aspect relates to our feelings of shock, sadness and occasionally guilt, depression and even denial. The physical area manifests in a more obvious way, perhaps crying, sickness, insomnia and an inability to concentrate. The cognitive side, which relates to the functioning of the brain, can give rise to self-blame, blame directed to others, a need to try and understand all aspects of the death and, specifically of interest in relation to horses, the timing of the decision to euthanize the animal. Finally, the social aspects may lead to self-isolation, incessant talking about the deceased animal or person and, on occasions, an urgency to find a replacement.

The degree to which people who work with racehorses, from stable staff to trainers and owners, cope with grief varies from person to person. Their responses to my enquiry about how they cope have ranged from the stoical and almost impassive 'just move on and get on with life' to accounts which have been at times incredibly moving.

People are right to remind us that the loss of a pet or animal is not as grave as the death of a human being, but the consequent effect on the person closest to the animal may be just as traumatic, perhaps in some cases even more so. As my father used to say, 'If it's important to that person, then it's important.'

Belinda Johnston, a veterinarian who has also trained as a counsellor, specialises in the human-companion animal relationship and offers emotional support for anyone who has lost a pet. Johnston runs a charitable organisation named 'Our Special Friends', through which she provides practical and emotional support in relation to the human/animal bond, especially in the elderly, vulnerable and socially isolated.

'Many people in the racing industry are in tune with their connectedness to animals,' she says, 'but I think there is also plenty of compassion fatigue, with people detaching themselves from what is happening in reality.'

Compassion fatigue, as the term implies, is a condition which is characterised by a gradual lessening of compassion over a period of time, commonly associated with people who work directly with trauma victims such as doctors, nurses and first responders. It has also been suggested that excessive coverage of stories of tragedy and suffering in the media can lead to compassion fatigue in society as a whole.

In one study it was found that up to 85 per cent of health care workers and just over a third of hospice nurses develop some form of compassion fatigue and people who develop this condition can exhibit symptoms of hopelessness, feelings of incompetency and self-doubt and an overall negative attitude. Racehorse professionals – trainers, owners and staff – may in some cases be prone to a type of compassion fatigue in their relationship with horses.

There are though, in the context of a racing stable, many factors which may affect the way those involved deal with the loss of a horse. Obviously the death of a horse can have a greater impact in a smaller yard than a large one, while the specific character of the horse must have a bearing. Most people will tell you they treat all horses the same regardless of their ability, but the loss of a well-known or top-class horse may resonate beyond the precincts of the industry.

One of the most recent high-profile deaths was when Gold Cup winner Synchronised suffered a freak accident in the 2012 Grand National. I was there and it was unquestionably one of the worst day's racing of my life. More importantly, with the eyes of the media firmly focused for those few minutes on the world's most famous race, it was a truly awful day for the industry.

This was a time when the focus on the race by animal rights bodies and the RSPCA was at its height. The previous year a global audience of 600 million people had seen the field switch to avoid the prostrate bodies of two horses that had suffered fatal falls – Ornais and Dooney's Gate – and there were serious doubts about the race's future survival.

Synchronised had fallen at Becher's first time round, unseating Tony McCoy, and galloped on riderless apparently unhurt. He continued to run free until attempting to jump the 11th fence, where he incurred a fracture of the tibia and fibula leaving the racecourse vets no option but to put him down.

Synchronised – one of AP McCoy's favourite horses

My other memory of that terrible day was hearing banshee-like wails echoing around the back of the stands in the aftermath of the race after the part-owner of According To Pete, a horse she had known since a foal, was told he had been fatally injured when brought down at Becher's. What made it even worse, as a media event, was that a few hours earlier the horse had been the subject of a TV insight piece by Clare Balding for the BBC.

Garage owner Peter Nelson, in whose colours the horse ran, said at the time: 'It's terrible. He was a family pet, part of the family. We've had loads of people knocking on the door, telephone calls, flowers and bottles of wine. But that doesn't bring him back does it? After the race we saw the loose horses running in and we were looking out for him, but he never came. It was devastating. We'd had him since he was a foal and we still have his mother. We had a stable at the back of the garage and a little paddock for him to run in.'

My only experience of losing a horse was when Cloudwalker, a grey who had won us a dozen races on the Flat and over jumps, took off a stride too soon at a fence down the far side at Market Rasen, landed awkwardly and sustained an injury to his pelvis. I was able to see him when he returned in the horse ambulance but feared the worst when the vet, who was knelt down examining him, turned his head to ask me if he was insured. The worst part of that day was the journey home with my trainer. It was very very quiet.

There are now organisations and people around to help owners cope with loss and, perhaps more important, the end-of-life decision. Belinda Johnston does so through 'Our Special Friends', and the British Horse Society has a scheme entitled 'Friends At The End'.

Most people who have been jump racing will have witnessed at some point the aftermath of a fatal injury to a horse. Ruth Carr speaks for many when she says:

'If I see a girl or lad return to the track with an empty bridle it brings a lump to my throat. I have been there and done it myself. It's a horrible thing. Imperial Djay had been a really good servant to us and got struck into. That was hard because it was at the races. You always hope that you can retire them, or find a new home or make the decision that the time has come, but it's always hard. We had to ring the girl from the races who looked after him. That was tough.'

'Imperial Djay liked to go out in a field and hated it if he didn't. He liked to stand on his own in the corner and for weeks after he died you would look out of the corner of your eye and think "Oh God, Djay isn't there".'

The late Jimmy FitzGerald, who trained 1,200 winners over a period of 33 years, enjoyed one of his greatest days when Forgive'n Forget won the 1985 Cheltenham Gold Cup. The horse was killed in the same race three years later. Ronnie Postlethwaite, a good friend, remembers the occasion: 'I went to Fitzy's yard for something and asked Jimmy how he was. He just looked at me and burst into tears. I said how awful it was and he just welled up. He was hard with people but not with horses.'

On top of the other unwelcome tasks demanded of a trainer following the death of a horse, a prime consideration is ensuring the staff, especially those closest to the horse, are able to cope.

Henrietta Knight, a former teacher and perhaps more mindful than some to the sensitivities of those around her, had to deal with a barrage of media interest when Best Mate collapsed and died of a heart attack at Exeter in late 2005.

Knight had handled Best Mate with great patience and skill, running him infrequently but having him trained to the minute to win three successive Cheltenham Gold Cups (2002, 2003 and 2004). He ran just twice in the season before his second and third triumphs, and in total appeared on the track just 22 times over a career stretching to seven seasons.

Best Mate – winner of three successive Gold Cups

Described by Knight as 'not one in a million, he's one in several million', Best Mate made his reappearance for the 2005/06 season in the William Hill Haldon Gold Cup Chase at Exeter on November 1. This was not a race he was expected to win, and he had already lost his place when his rider pulled him up before the third last. A few minutes later he collapsed near the final fence, having suffered from what proved a fatal heart attack.

In spite of the flurry of activity all around her in the hours or two after Best Mate's death, notably trying to comfort the horse's distraught owner Jim Lewis, Knight knew from her many years of experience that one of the toughest things for the staff to overcome is the sight of the empty box. Seven years is a long time in any walk of life, and there would be lads and lasses back home aware that there would be one less mouth to feed that evening.

Knight told me: 'When you have staff working for you then you have to be strong. You can't collapse in a heap. You have to brace yourself but I rang home and had Red Blazer put into Best Mate's box the evening of the day he died.'

In doing this Knight displayed a sensitivity and understanding of the feelings of her staff, just as Paul Nicholls had with Clifford Baker following the tragic death of his son. Sometimes the lot of a racehorse trainer encompasses rather more than mere equine husbandry.

Oliver Sherwood is also aware that there are staff at home that may need support when a horse, especially an old favourite, is lost. 'It's tough. It's the hardest thing, but as a leader of a team you have lads, lasses and other horses to look after the next morning. Most owners know that it is harder for the lad or lass. There is nothing worse than having one runner at the races and the travelling lad or lass has to come back to an empty box, or seeing a lad or lass in floods of tears holding the tack. Eric's Charm broke my heart. He was like part of the family.'

Eric's Charm – much loved by all who knew him

David Pipe and his father before him have had many top-class horses through their hands, but one horse David had a special fondness for was Salut Flo. He had joined the yard from France and ran just five times for him, winning very easily on his UK debut at Doncaster in March, 2010, and then landing the prestigious Byrne Group Plate at the 2012 Cheltenham Festival.

'It hit us hard when we lost him because he was very very tough. He had colic but fought to the bitter end to try and stay alive. Other horses would have died two or three days earlier. It was a tough one losing him.'

Paul Nicholls still has fond memories of Twist Magic, who won 10 of his 30 races including the 2007 and 2009 runnings of the Tingle Creek Chase.

'He was an awesome horse,' says Nicholls. 'He was a character – we did have a few little issues and battles with him trying to get him to start – but he was very very good but broke his neck at Newbury. That was an absolutely dreadful day. We still think of him now two or three years later. Every time we have a Grade 1 winner – and he won five – I put up a plaque and Twist Magic's name is now immortal in our yard. Up there in lights so we all see it every day.'

Henry Candy, who has trained horses for over 40 years, is also renowned for his gentle and patient approach to training. He says: 'I am probably one of the soppiest trainers around. It is horrible when they die. It is like losing a dog or even a friend. I would not want to train jumpers for that reason. The one consolation is that after a while you realise how little pain an animal sometimes feels compared with a human. You see a horse with a broken leg eating grass. It is when they cool down that the pain gets greater. Their pain threshold is very different.'

Thankfully horses with life-threatening injuries are despatched relatively quickly these days. Roger Charlton says: 'If a horse dies you have to blank it out. The worst is when a horse breaks a leg on the gallops and you have to hold it and wait for someone to come and put it down. You just hope they are not feeling it. That is the tough bit.'

Despite living and working with horses for over six decades Willie Carson readily admits he still struggles.

'It's harder with the passing of years. The older I get the softer I get. I didn't like it but I used to be able to hold a horse if it was going to be put down. I'm the boss now but when they are putting down an old mare I make some excuse and go.'

Peter Makin also finds it especially hard to deal with the loss of a mare. 'It gets no easier to bear, but we have lost very few horses. We have been very lucky. I would have said half a dozen, no more. One of the worst things is having to put an old mare down. That always upsets me.'

William Haggas prefers not to be around when the moment arrives. 'I lost a filly called Chain Of Jewels owned by Cheveley Park. She broke her leg and I was distraught when she was put down. That was really early on in my training career.'

He recalls one harrowing experience in France. 'My wife Maureen had a great affinity with a filly she rode all the time called Dever Dream. She fractured her leg in the Prix de la Foret at Longchamp. They were a shambles at the racecourse and they took ages to help her. They didn't give her enough anaesthetic and she was in agony. Maureen has probably never got over it. We wanted her put down as soon as possible but they took ages. She will stand with them when they have to be put down. I can't do that I'm afraid.'

As an experienced veterinarian Dermot Weld had to make life and death decisions for animals on many occasions. Yet he talks movingly about the final hours.

'I had a two-year-old recently. He had a few little problems before I got him and he broke a leg. We tried to save him and got him to the veterinary surgery which is here beside me. He was a gorgeous tempered animal but died in my arms. He had a very bad fracture but would not have felt much pain because his nerve supply had been ruptured. I became a vet because I wanted to save animals. I would have preferred to become an equine surgeon. But as a trainer I have to combine toughness and a will to win with sensitivity. They have to meet in the middle. Training racehorses keeps you very humble and very sane.'

John Oxx also qualified as a veterinarian. He says: 'It's part of the game. I have horses for shorter periods of time than most people as my clients are big sellers. It must be harder for someone who trains a 10-year-old jumper. That must be devastating. We don't lose many but it is hard when it happens and affects the owner more. It goes with the territory. I qualified as a vet and I have seen that side. It is a difficult phone call to the owner. The main thing is that the horse doesn't suffer and a quick decision is made.'

Dan Skelton describes some of the emotions associated with the grieving process, notably the cognitive side relating to self-blame and trying to understand the process better.

'You never like to think too much about it but it does sometimes creep into your mind that it is ages since you lost one. It is part of the job though. If you have livestock you will get deadstock. Whether it is greyhound racing, pigeon racing, farming, animal husbandry, pets – where there are live ones there will be dead ones. I've lost horses on the track and at home and it doesn't make it any easier to deal with. It's horrible and leaves you numb.

'I experience a feeling of helplessness and ask what I could have done. But the consolation is that I helped make the horse happy and gave it a great life. We can send one out there and an accident happens. It's no different to leaving your front gate open and thinking you have shut it and the dog runs out and gets killed. You don't stop breeding dogs.'

Sir Mark Prescott puts forward a well-reasoned argument in defence of those who work closely with horses in the racing industry.

'The horse is a working animal. I think modern man has lost all understanding of this. Forty or 50 years ago the countryman under-stood this. On the farm our duty is to look after the animal as well as we can but it is a fact that we are going to kill it one day, either so we can eat the meat or somebody can wear leather shoes. What you owe them is the very very best life you can give them and either a natural or speedy end. That is the deal. When the sheepdog can't round them up any more you put him down. He was not kept as a pet. As soon as a chicken can't fly up to its perch it is killed that night by a fox or a stoat. As soon as it can't roost that's it. That is the law of nature. In nature there is no need for nursing homes.'

Dan Skelton also alludes to the animal kingdom: 'It's like the lioness in the Serengeti. If she has six cubs and one goes missing she does not abandon the other five to find the one. They look after the five, have to find food and move on. That is the instinct. A human will go "Oh my God" if that happened. If a mother lost her daughter she probably wouldn't eat for a week. Even though we have domesticated all these animals we can't get away from their instincts.'

Jim Bolger became accustomed to loss from an early age. 'I never found it that difficult because I grew up with that kind of loss. My father used to say that growing up on a farm is a great experience. I am not the first person to say it but when you have animals you will have loss. I knew all the cows on our farm individually – where they came from and sometimes how much they cost – and when one died my father said "as long as we can keep it outside the home we will cope". That was how he dealt with it. It was not such a big deal as long as the loss was kept outside the home.

'I am quick to put animals down rather than see them suffer for a few days because they are not going to come back and the decision has to be made fairly quickly.'

John Francome remembers the 1977 Cheltenham Festival, when his yard lost Lanzarote after he broke a leg in the Gold Cup and Bula in the Queen Mother Champion Chase. The two had won three Champion Hurdles between them: 'You are not going to live forever. You have livestock and you have deadstock. When I was with Fred Winter we lost Bula and Lanzarote at the same Festival. They both had good lives. You have to get up and go.'

Peter Scudamore also thinks it through pragmatically.

'If I have a moral dilemma it is that racehorses are better looked after than humans. If a horse breaks its leg on the track then within a few minutes it is dead. Putting horses down is not cruel. Putting them in a field when it's wet and cold can be in certain circumstances.

Death is something that an animal senses in a different way to us. It is not possible to save all the animals in the world. It is awful when an animal dies, but it can be catastrophic when the life of a human being is lost.'

Nobody reading this book will be immune from grief. A fortnight before my father was to die from a serious coronary I visited him in hospital. The consultant found a moment to take me to one side for a 'quiet word' about my father's condition, in which he expressed grave concerns about the prognosis. Put bluntly, he told me that my father was going to die.

I walked back into the ward, tried to put on a brave face, but my father was a man of great intuition and he quickly sensed that something was up. I told him that he would need to take things easy for a while. 'Oh, call it a day then?' he replied, alluding to his life as a parish priest. Within moments I saw that something had changed. It was as if the spirit had left him.

I caught the bus home and found myself overcome with grief. Tears welled up in my eyes when someone – I don't even remember looking round to see who it was – put their hand on my shoulder and said, quietly, 'You'll be all right, don't worry.'

That was my time for grieving. I didn't see my father again. He died ten days later, but due to that experience on the bus I found that I was better equipped to handle the news when it came. I had been through what is referred to in bereavement counselling as anticipatory grief.

That process helped me manage the moment of my father's death better than had it come unexpectedly. People who work in racing don't always have that advantage. Sometimes it will be known that a horse may have to be euthanized, but for horses lost in a race or through an accident at home there is no opportunity for early grieving.

Michael Dickinson experienced the loss of a horse both as a rider and trainer: 'I have always been totally ill-equipped to deal with the loss of any horse. This was especially true when I was a National Hunt jockey because I was always cognisant of the fact that I was only winning races because of the horses. The National Hunt horses we often had for several years. I was with them every day through the summer and winter and when I was riding them in novice chases the bonding was strong. It still hurts me today when I think of some of the horses I rode that died in a race. It has not become easier with the passing of time.'

I have spoken to many people who work closely with horses about dealing with loss. Luca Cumani says: 'You never become desensitized. It is the worst thing that can happen. They all hurt and you don't make distinctions. If you lose a horse it's a loss you feel for a number of days.'

In some cases it can last longer. Alan Bailey rode many top-class performers at home for Peter Walwyn, but the horse for whom he had the greatest fondness was Be Hopeful – the first horse Walwyn trained – who died in a freak accident at the age of 14.

'I sobbed like a baby,' he told me. 'I came into the house minutes after he had been put down. I came in for breakfast but I was ashen and my wife Jan asked what was wrong. I just broke down and sobbed like a child. He broke a leg on the shavings gallop. He had never been lame in his life. They put a plaster cast on but he'd never had one on before and he lunged forward over some bales and then broke the other leg.

'I rode him every day and he was a lovely horse. I used to get him in his box and say "You old bastard Hoppy ..." He would have his ears flat back and you would chase him round the box. I could do anything with him. He was a wonderful horse. One of the first sentences my daughter said was "Come on Hoppy ..." He used to go home every winter and was well fed and cared for, but when he came back he was covered in cow muck and mud. It hung around him like the coat of a grizzly bear. When the weather was changing one day you would go in and pull it all off. Mind you he could jump and kick.

'People don't believe this when I tell them but we had muck sacks in those days and one day he saw me and grabbed the sack and I went arse over tit. I could swear he was laughing when I looked round at him. That horse could do everything but talk.'

Bailey left the room for a few moments and returned with a hoof, smartly varnished bearing a silver plaque with the name Be Hopeful. 'The owner Mrs Williams gave me that. You know those sales last week where that Arab paid all that money for a yearling? Not even he could afford to buy that from me.'

Racehorses are, like every living being, at risk. Things go wrong, either at home or on the track. They grow old and become infirm. Those who are entrusted with responsibility for them, either as trainers, owners or stable staff, have a duty of care to provide for them as best they can while they are with us. Their death ends a life – not a relationship.

A racehorse lives in the moment. Our duty, when possible, is to allow it to die in one.

Index

Page numbers in italics refer to illustrations.

Picture Acknowledgements

Photographs

Beha Anthony/Sipa: page 37 top

Caroline Norris: pages 24, 70

Gerry Cranham: pages 131, 146, 159, 184

Getty Images: pages 43, 109

Grossick Racing: page 53, 119, 160

Hugh Routledge: page 4

Jack Dixon: back flap

Mark Cranham: pages 36, 112

Marten Julian: pages xii, 166

Martyn Lynch: page 17

Racing Post/Edward Whitaker: pages xiv, 10, 12, 14, 18, 19, 37 bottom, 44, 50, 65, 67, 76, 88, 98, 102, 121, 128, 139, 148, 151, 152, 172, 174, 182, 186, back cover bottom

Racing Post/Patrick McCann: pages 57, 63, 74, 86

Rosalie Winard: page 61

Illustrations

Darren Bird: pages 29, 92, 129